For Barry
with all good silver wishes
From the author
and her manager
November 2012
Gertrude.

Gertrude M. Marsh

Gertrude M. marsh

Saints, Ships and Suspense

My Norwegian Pilgrimage

ⴟ tapir academic press

Dedication:

This book is affectionately dedicated to my

First Norwegian Guide and Friend

ØRNULF NORMANN NORGÅRD

now my

Dearest Friend and Fellow Pilgrim

Dendrobium ØRNULF NORGÅRD
"Gertrude"
Singapore Botanic Gardens 2009

Layout: Mari Røstvold, Tapir Academic Press
Paper: Artic Volume 115 g
Printed and bound by AIT Otta AS

Art work on cover:
Rebecca Heaton-Cooper (Great grand-daughter of Alfred Heaton Cooper)

Tapir Academic Press publishes textbooks and academic literature for universities and university colleges, as well as for vocational and professional education. We also publish high quality literature of a more general nature. Our main product lines are:

- *Textbooks for higher education*
- *Research and reference literature*
- *Non-fiction*

We only use environmentally certified printing houses.

Tapir Academic Press
NO–7005 Trondheim, Norway
Tel.:   + 47 73 59 32 10
Email: forlag@tapir.no
www.tapirforlag.no

Contents

Foreword

By the Way

Come with me, at an octogenarian's pace in a jet propelled age, as I recall some of the interesting and fascinating things, I have encountered on my pilgrimage of life.

On the completion of my first book, 'A Vivid Shaft of Northern Light', I determinedly stated I would never write another but I was curious about one thing. Where did Bishop Johan Ernst Gunnerus actually die on 25 September 1773? One thing led to another, to further inquiries, to revisits ... even from pole to pole. I am no erudite scholar but I am determined. I have enjoyed searching, recalling the little things of life, the chance encounters, the making of new friends and the cementing of old.

Let us journey on together and recover some of the often missed or forgotten ordinary, little things of life which support the great, as I have discovered mainly in the unique country of Norway, Scandinavia, the north-west corner of Europe.

Gertrude M. Marsh
Singapore, Lillehammer 2002 - 2009.

Notes

- Norwegian words are italicized.
- Latin words are italicized.
- Quotes are italicized.
- The definite article in Norwegian is *-en* or *-et* at the end of a noun.
  Example *bre* (glacier); *bre<u>en</u>* (the glacier);
  plural *-er*
  definite; plural *-ene breene* (the glaciers); breer (glaciers)

Introduction: The Tale of an Explorer

It has been said, you will even find it condensed in a German proverb, that when travelling you do not return with more than you left. A surprising and somewhat paradoxical drop of wisdom this is, but I find it reflected and solved in the travels you are invited to join in this book. As Gertrude M. Marsh takes us travelling through landscapes, society and history - mostly in Norway - we learn and we do return with more than at the outset. This is partly due to the fact that Gertrude stands out as an outstanding connoisseur of facts and flavours of the many but still carefully chosen aspects of history, nature and contemporary society she guides us through.

The book is a synthesis that in terms of actual travels covers a period of close to 60 years. As invited followers we are enlightened. But this book is not the conventional traveller's guide; neither does it follow the format of a classical travel narrative. This book is driven by the reason for travelling - the why - and the skill to observe and synthesize for a purpose. It is the 'why' that is the key to the routes and the meticulously chosen observations and reflections along the road. 'Why' is in its essence particular and personal, making this a personal text but never private. As a personal undertaking it is inviting and inspiring, and nowhere excluding.

The 'why' of the undertaking is not easily summed up without risking to dislocate or disturb a focus or thread by readers who come to this text with other experience or anticipation than me. In fact, one of the beauties of the text is that you can join the journey and find ample room for your own observations and reflections in the text.

This is a book about Norway, its culture and history, its geography and everyday life and manners as the author has seen it develop through the many travels countrywide since the early 1950-ties. And this book is about the strong bonds that exist between Scandinavia and The British Isles - and especially Norway and England. The latter not presented as grand history or politics, but in nature and living culture through time and the eyes of the author.

The text is conceived in love for countries and scenes, but love has not made the author blind. By drawing on a battery of perspectives - botany, horticulture, culture - sea and mountain, history, geography, architecture and more - she takes us to a deeper and well composed understanding of the places along the route; a route which pretty much covers the 2500 km long Norwegian coast from Oslo to Kirkenes.

Geiranger 1952.

And why is this route and these places chosen? This reveals yet another layer in the text. The author sets out to solve a puzzle in Norwegian history: Exactly where did Norway's prominent bishop Johan Ernst Gunnerus die? The author has in a previous book written extensively about Gunnerus in "*A Vivid Shaft of Northern Light. Journeys with Bishop Johan Ernst Gunnerus and Flora Norvegica through three centuries*" (2002). In the present book her will to communicate understanding of Norway melts in with the desire to follow the bishop on his travels to its final stop. She succeeds. The hunt for the death bed of Johan Ernst Gunnerus acts both as an essential purpose of the travels in itself and as a warp into which she has woven her picture of the country.

So the traveller becomes a shuttle and the author a drive picker - and how appropriate. For what is man but a traveller - and certainly so in a very concrete sense in our times. The share volume of travelling is surging in contemporary society, which brings me back to the paradoxes of travel and the drop of wisdom in the proverb. Now we can see the message in the apparent paradox and appreciate the importance of this book: Travel *per se* does not make a man wiser, travel can easily be made into superficial consumerism. To be enriched by travel the traveller must nourish a receptacle and a will to fill it by listening in to and making a fabric from the many channels of communication that a culture and society speaks through - and never stop exploring. This brings us, I suspect, to the epicenter of the author's enterprise, it is the enterprise of an explorer - an explorer searching for identity and structure in a flux. This is a universal importance of the book, for if man is a traveller, the book presents us with a way to reach the ultimate goal of exploration, the hearts and deeds of mankind.

Tor Arnesen
Lillehammer July 2009

Author (centre) waiting for lunch with two cousins, Sogndal August 1952.

Norway

NORTH
SEA.

SWEDEN

FINLAND

NORDKAP

KIRKENES

ALTA

·KARASJOK

·KAUTOKEINO

HARSTAD

SVOLVÆR

Å

BODØ

MO I RANA

SANDNESSJØEN

BRØNNØYSUND

·NAMSOS

KRISTIANSUND   TRONDHEIM

·ÅLESUND ·ÅNDALSNES

STAD   GEIRANGER

·STRYN

RØROS

SOGNEFJORDEN

BERGEN   HARDANGER

OSLO

·STAVANGER   LARVIK

·KRISTIANSAND

My Pilgrimage

I stood alone on the edge of the world. It was a place I had longed to find, to just - be! Most noticeable was the music of silence harmoniously enveloping me. I never even thought of the mighty roar of the colourful, constantly moving traffic of the modern city where I reside. I was aware of a soft, pervasive, lovely peace surrounding me, in contrast to the din of daily life. I am not sure if I took a deep breath first to grasp afresh the newness of nature or held my breath in an attempt to clasp a fleeting moment.

My feet were on a plateau of firm ground blanketed with soft, cropped, green turf sprinkled with the tiniest *Alchemilla alpina* (English -Lady's mantle; Norwegian- *Fjellmarikåpe*) I have ever seen. Stay a moment, it can only be examined on the knees. A telephoto lens was inappropriate. It was only 2cm tall and I could not see to count the flower clusters never mind the individual petals and the lobes of leaves. On further consideration I believe it could have been *Aphanes inexspectata*, Dwarf, or pygmy, lady's mantle; (Norwegian - *Dvergmarikåpe*); for this is only 3-10 cm and found in rare spots of the western fjords, though more prevalent in Denmark.

Stad, the most westerly point of Norway.

Alchemilla alpina
Lady's Mantle (English)
Fjellmarikåpe (Norwegian)

Before me, as I gazed to the west, was the vast Atlantic Ocean. The waves today had playful, white plumed crests. There was no hint of the fierce heavy grey breakers that have wreaked damage along this coast for millions of years. As my eyes lowered to the edge of the green carpet, the result of that restless, battering action was seen, in the small rocky islands, the skerries, which form a protective barrier for a few thousand kilometres along the north-west coast of Norway. Here it is a rampart of cliff and a thundering ocean current.

Beyond the steep cliff and the skerries, this day I had an undisturbed view over an undulating blue and silver ocean to the Færoe Islands. On the far horizon were mountains of ethereal, grey-blue, the same shape as the one on which I stood. I was on the exact same latitude as the Færoe Islands and looking out from the tip of the Stadland peninsula, the most westerly point of Norway, I imagined I could vaguely see the North American continent.

This was certainly a rare golden-blue day blending to give the luscious green immediately beneath and around me. It could just have easily been a wet, windy, grey day with fog-bound coast and skerries, impossible to see a shore-line below and the satin blue shimmering sheet, a thunderous onslaught of relentless waves of molten steel. Soft as silk or strong as iron, the constant pulsing beat of the Atlantic Ocean was carrying the warmer water from the equatorial stream of the Gulf of Mexico to the coast of Norway, creating this unique land of *fjord*, *fjell* and *foss*, with its distinctive coastline.

We pay a penalty for this warm salt-water. So often the warm, westerly, moisture bearing winds of the Atlantic are forced upwards, as they meet the Arctic barrier of perpetual ice and so deposit their dampness on us, especially as they try to escape southwards towards Bergen, Scotland and the English Channel. (A Bergen taxi driver once told me that when God created Bergen he considered it so beautiful he sent rain every day to keep it fresh and clean.)

Thank God for the mist and dampness, for it is this North Atlantic Drift which maintains the deeply indented coast of Norway ice free, with the lines of transport and communication open throughout the year and produces verdant green pasture covering rocky ledges for food and thought.

Today is a perfect day in early September with a high dome of deepest ice- blue, supported by mountain pillars of grey greens, blue, and distant shady mauve, the colours blending together in range upon range of mountains from north east to south west.

I turn to the left, away from the ocean, and as I stare southwards over Western Norway, the old, old mountainous block gashed by wind, ice and water into long, deep crevices, alternately supplying and receiving energy and debris from the land and sea, ice-age to ice age, forming the fjords of today, I am transported in time.

You cannot help feeling history here. Looking down from a satellite the peninsula stretches out from a narrow isthmus like a great animal's forelimb, its right paw graspingly open with its five claws covetously extended into the sea. There is no doubt the sailors of old felt this avaricious drag on many occasions, for they sheltered weeks in Sildegapet or Skårfjorden awaiting calmer water to round the West Cape. The very name 'Stad' means 'stay'.

Some seamen were so impatient to avoid this perilous stretch of sea they would drag their boat over the isthmus to be on their way. I

Skerries, small rocky islands.

Glimpse of Nordfjord looking inland to south east.

Pause on Kjerringa (The old lady) with Rondane mountains and Dovre in background.

Sildegapet and part of the drag way.

Selje village, Stad.

walked part of this drag way that glorious September day, for it is still evident, with ancient timber in places to ease the movement of the vessel, to the stone cross at Dragseidet. The granite cross marks the spot where Olav Tryggvason, blown off course for Bergen when returning from exile in England, forcibly baptised the Norwegians Christian in 995 AD – ancient peer pressure! He continued his journey north-eastwards to establish the city of Trondheim in 997.

The left limb of our imaginary animal is more relaxed, almost enclosing Sildegapet and so protecting the precious small island of Selje, the most sacred spot in Western Norway. It was to this uninhabited green island in the legendary past that the boats, containing an Irish princess and her attendants, drifted.

There are several accounts of the arrival of Sunniva and her weary companions onto this isolated island. Although clothed in legend and history we should not dismiss the story for recent years of exploration, scientific investigation and academic research have often revealed some small truth in the stories of the past. I find well written and deeply researched material in the Norwegian Nobel Laureate Sigrid Undset's (1882 - 1949) works. So I turned to her version of the establishment of the community and subsequent events on Selje. She herself lived on the island for some time absorbing the atmosphere whilst writing. We shall feel much more of Sigrid Undset's aptitude to make the past alive later in our journey as we reach Gudbrandsdalen.

Sunniva was the eldest daughter of a mid-tenth century Christian king (chief) of a small kingdom in Ireland. Educated in the cloisters of the abbey on the estate she had determined, from being a child, to devote her life to Christ, hoping to eventually become abbess.

On the death of her father Sunniva became ruler and the inhabitants looked to her wisdom and knowledge for guidance and protection. Several small kingdoms had been taken over by marriage and here was an ideal opportunity, a desirable girl ruling a well organised community. Never wavering from her early vow, she called her local council (*Ting*) together, informed them of her rejection of all non-Christian proposals and handed over the complete control of the kingdom to them. She herself would leave by boat, without sails or oars, confidently trusting the God she had promised to serve to lead her to a place of refuge.

Three ships left the Irish coast to drift with the current through the outer isles of Britain, for Sunniva had invited any of her people who wished to join her and many men and women pledged themselves to God and the popular, pious princess. Around Pentland Firth and the Isles of Orkney land was seen in the murky distance only to disappear until eventually they approached shelter in Firdafylke in Western Norway, to a hostile reception.

The few families along the narrow coastal strip were fishermen/ farmers barely eking a living from the sea and mountains. They were afraid of visitors from the sea and these three ships must have looked like pirate wrecks with hungry, wild men on board after the North Sea storms. Turning from the greeting of stones and arrows the travellers returned to the main stream to face further storms and the tiny fleet was split, one ship being stranded on the island of Kinn, north of Sognefjord. These voyagers inhabited the island and there may even be descendants there today. They would be the likely eye witnesses and reporters of the later events on Selje.

There were no resident people on the island of Selje when the remainder of the party drifted on to a rocky beach. Shelter was

On the west front of Nidaros Cathedral. Statues of St. Sunniva (left) and St. Olav.

Pollen, Stad.

The stone cross at Dragseidet.

Here Olav Tryggvason foreibly baptised the Norwegians in 995 AD.

immediately available in the natural caves formed by inclinations of the predominant slabs of slate. The sparse pasture land had been used in the summer by local farmers for grazing cattle and horses but no one lived there.

Sunniva and her companions soon made a simple church within a cave well above the shore line and improved their dwelling accommodation. Their diet consisted mainly of fish, easily harvested from Sildegapet, the extensive bay around the island, famous for its seasonal shoals of herring.

When the summer came and the local farmers wished to occupy their traditional pastures, they jealously suspected the settlers were pirates or thieves about to steal their animals. They rallied round the local lord, Haakon Jarl and attacked the peaceful occupants. Knowing of the ferocity of the invaders Sunniva and the innocent group entered their church and prayed for safety in God's power so the heathens would not take them.

There was a rock fall as the war-like men approached and the entrance to the church was sealed.

Many years later, a century or more, local residents noticed a rare light coming from the island and reflected in the sea. They rowed out to investigate and found the base of the light on a snowy white skull and a strange, smooth sweet atmosphere pervaded the vicinity. The skull was taken to Olav Tryggvason (963-1000) and Bishop Sigurd in Trondheim who considered it a holy relic.

King Olav Tryggvason (Olav I) called a *Ting*, a gathering of local chiefs, at Dragseidet where he forced baptism on the men and then asked about Selje. He visited the island and noticed there had been a recent rock avalanche and many bones were found between the stones. Beneath an overhanging rock he found many stones. He forced his way in and eventually found the complete body of Sunniva 'as if sleeping'.

King Olav I had the first church built on the site of the cave. Early in the twelfth century King Eystein I built an abbey on the island dedicated to St Alban. Sunniva was beatified and as the Patron Saint of *Vestlandet* (Western Norway) her shrine was placed on the high altar of the newly completed cathedral in the developing city of Bergen in 1170.

Pasture land near St. Olav's cross.

A millennium later, with my back to the Atlantic Ocean, from the summit of 'the Old Lady' (*Kjerringa*), I turn and face the Romsdal Alps with their mighty peaks and gaze in fascination over this area, the inspiring county of *Møre og Romsdal* (Møre and Romsdal), steeped in history. It is a district of contrasting surprises from the pockets of Mediterranean type climate producing flowers, fruit, vegetables and I guess, the most delicious hay the cows could ruminate upon; they certainly looked contented near St Olav's cross; to steep, stony mountain peaks, the delight of skilled, indomitable climbers.

Almost full circle and I scanned the northern Atlantic and thought of the variety of boats and ships, in peace and war, in joy and sorrow, the ocean had carried. The **Hurtigruten**, the express coastal ships, continue to pass this stretch of sometimes vicious water, twice a day, once in each direction, keeping well away from the notorious promontory although often snaking their way feelingly through narrow sounds, with pride. What a joy to be transported in a modern vessel of today, compared with my first journey fifty years

West Cape in the far distance.

The Norwegian Travel Agent in London 1964.

ago. The ships still serve the same purpose, working vessels joining people and places, but they have changed with the time and tide. What changes!

Here at West Cape (*Vestkapp*) I could rest in perfect peace. It has escaped the commercialisation of North Cape with its attendant crowd and coaches. I have long wanted to stand, like the gigantic figure of Rollo (Rolf the Ganger), the Viking in Ålesund, looking out towards the open sea and imagine Viking craft gathering in sheltered creeks before some mighty expeditions a thousand years ago.

It is recorded that there were many ships from Vestlandet included amongst the two hundred vessels King Harald Hardråde (1015-1066) amassed here before sailing from Herdlafjorden to conquer England in 1066. There was a savage fight at Stamford Bridge on the River Ouse near York. The Viking invaders were defeated and Harald Hardråde killed on 25th September. Immediately King Harold of England had to remarshall his troops and rush to the south of England to defend his realm from the Normans under William, Duke of Normandy, a descendant of the famous Norseman Rollo whose figure we noted in Ålesund. So Viking ancestry conquered England at the Battle of Hasting on 14th October 1066.

My very first Norwegian friends, the staff of Norwegian State Railways in London, who did such a wonderful job after the Second World War in arranging and publicising travel in Norway, used to tease me as a Yorkshire lass that I had been left behind at the Battle of Stamford Bridge. I wonder?

For many years, as I visited and studied Norway, I desired to explore this western tip which no tour included. There was always some excuse when I enquired about the possibility - weather, closed roads, resurfacing and 'not quite sure how to get there' ... But today I had a driver who had an intimate knowledge of the byways of the area and a third generation hotelier kind enough to supply a most comfortable vehicle to make it possible to attain my goal.

I pondered here on my affinity for Norway. How had my interest developed? Why should I be attached to this unique country in this special way? It has had a peculiar attraction for me from childhood, as though born in me, yet my family had no known connection. Here I stood alone on this mountain plateau between ocean and rugged terrain. I had just left Nidaros Cathedral, determined to find more traces of **Johan Ernst Gunnerus,** the bishop from 1758 to his death on a pastoral visitation in 1773. I was disappointed to find very few people knew of this bishop whose scientific work in the realms of nature, was almost forgotten. I could not even ascertain, from usually well documented sources, where he died.

JOHAN ERNST GUNNERUS
1718–1773.
Bishop of Trondheim 1758–1773.

I unexpectedly met Gunnerus (1718 - 1773) in an antiquarian book shop in 1997 when I was searching for a book on Norwegian flora. I found that the first published collection of such was by J.E.Gunnerus in 1776. It was not what I needed. I wanted a modern coloured dictionary of plant life, for I had been exiled in the tropics for twenty years. Now a widow, I was alone, free to take up interests of my childhood and visit my beloved Norway. As I turned the pages of **Flora Norvegica** I realised I had found a treasure and a kindred spirit. The work of the first biography of Bishop Gunnerus in English was published but I could not let him go. From the peace of Stad I started my pilgrimage.

Two original sketches from the unpublished notebook of Alfred Heaton Cooper (1863–1929)
of the sea-cliff. Hornelen c. 1900.
By kind permission of the Heaton-Cooper Studio, Grasmere

Nordfjord

From the most westerly tip of the Norwegian coast, resting on the summit of Kjerringa, I look over the Stadland peninsula, my attention ever drawn to the distant mountains. Directly south is the shadowy, pointed shape of the 860m peak of Hornelen and I chuckle to myself as I recall some of the fantastic stories told of mysterious exploits and happenings said to have taken place there on Midsummer's eves, when the witches danced and even kings raced.

Before Hornelen is a linear, deep shadow indicating the course of the Nordfjord from the widespread Jostedalsbreen, one of the most extensive remains of bygone Ice Ages in Europe and its many off-shoots. In the foreground a few royal-blue ribbon strips of fjord waters smilingly (on a sunny day) reveal the main Nordfjord. In the far, far distance the rounded domes of the Jotunheimen, the home of the giants (or trolls), lazily gaze towards the azure haze above. This block of mountains, from east to south across the corner of our panorama, forms a division between the fjords of Western Norway and the great Eastern Valley.

We turn from the western extremity to the deep cleft of the Nord-fjord with the Hornelen sea cliff, the highest sea cliff in Northern

Europe, striving to stretch its pinnacle higher from its almost island base. Turning inland, eastwards, the road closely adjoins the fjord shore along the narrow coastal strip emphasizing the importance of the waterway from time immemorial. An ancient stone cross, on a narrow, tree sheltered slope between the road and the fjord, is thought to mark the site of a religious gathering place likely dating from the tenth or eleventh century.

We certainly witnessed modern changes in the way of living. By a stone dwelling the farmer's wife was waiting to open a five-barred gate across the steep entrance to the farm. She was waiting for her husband returning from the *seter*, the summer pasture, bringing the cows and goats. Now not only was this an unusual occurrence, the male to be bringing the cattle and the woman waiting at the farm, but he was bringing them by tractor – motorised transport!

Only a couple of centuries ago – you can tell I am getting old - three months' of summer work on the farm would have occupied four or five women and girls living up on the mountain pastures. As soon as the snow had receded from the mountain, uncovering fresh, luscious herbage, the jolly procession would leave the home farm. There would be excitement for all participants, leaving the confines of the dark winter and climbing up towards the sunlit heights of summer for there is only a very short spring in the mountains. The steep, stony path would be negotiated upwards with happiness for there was freedom for humans and animals ahead.

Thrusting its way, seemingly through solid ground, would be seen a small clump of tiny citron yellow flowers, coltsfoot (*Tussilago farfara*, Norwegian *Hestehov*). First the small tightly folded flower bud shoots its way, almost unnoticed, from its root system through

10th/11th century meeting place on Nordfjord.

Tussilago farfara (latin). Hestehov (Norwegian). Coltsfoot.

the outer layer, upwards to the light, like a bullet penetrating metal and then unfolds its welcoming colour on a short grey stem which has burst through protective furry sheaths. It is only after the flower fades that the tooth-edged heart shaped leaves are seen round the base of the stem. I have seen coltsfoot push through hard surfaced road edges and could not help wondering at its remarkable energy – the new life of spring. It would be gathered by the young Gunnerus, for its medicinal properties have been known for generations, as a soothing cough medicine and a substitute for tobacco.

There was much to do on arrival at the *seter* for rarely had anyone been there during the snow bound winter months. Minor repairs may be needed where the melting snow had seeped through, refreshing the bed straw where some unexpected tiny visitors had made their nest, and seeing that the animals were fed and watered - a very busy time needing springtime energy. Eventually they would create a routine, caring for the animals and preparing cream, butter and cheese, some to be sent down to the farm weekly but mainly for winter supplies. If there was suitable land available a few crops and vegetables would be cultivated, growing quickly in the long midsummer days without nights. The grasses were the most important for without the hay for winter fodder more animals would have to be slaughtered. Look upwards today and you will see how the remaining high summer farms which survive at all, are surrounded by steep, stony uneven pastures which have to be cut by hand.

I remember seeing the farmer cut the grass on his turf roof for hay in Geiranger as the Eagle Road was being made in August 1952. Nearby on a flat shelf-like area on the mountain side four poles had been erected equidistant with three lengths of wire stretched across them. The cut hay was thrown over the wires, like washing

Nordfjord

Stone farm building and elderberry tree.

Nordpollen

This roof produces hay. I have seen goats tethered on it too.

on a line to dry, well off the ground for the night dews could delay drying.

Some time would be found for collecting berries, herbs and medicinal plants, needed at home. The high days would be when the young men came up from the farm on a Saturday night to collect the produce of the week and take it back to the home farm ready for taking to market or manor.

Young Johan Ernst Gunnerus from 1722 onwards (he was born in Christiania 1718) would delight to go with his medical doctor father to collect plants, roots, seeds, tree bark to take home to his mother to prepare for pharmaceutical use. It is from those happy days Johan Ernst's interest and knowledge of botany and natural history developed. Here too may have been laid the basis of his extraordinary knowledge of and ability in the use of Latin. That was a century after the Reformation and church services were no longer in Latin. Now, even three hundred years later, doctors' prescriptions are written mainly in Latin, if you can read them.

Packing up and making all secure in the *seter* in late summer would be a long wearisome business. The journey down the mountain could be treacherous, especially if autumn had come earlier than anticipated. Now the cattle were brought down by truck. It would be like being taken through a busy airport in the comfort of a wheelchair or would the cattle be nervous of a new experience?

Nordfjord is particularly deep once over the threshold of islands protecting the mouth of the fjord like teeth. The fjord became popular as wealthy foreign private ship owners escaped the developing industrial areas of Britain and Europe in the later days of the nineteenth century, and explored inland Norway by the waterways. Some would anchor at Nordfjordeid, still a north-south and east-west cross roads, but the adventurous would take the stream and make for the inner reaches of the fjord, especially Innvik leading into Utvik. The deepest point of the fjord (565m) is where the Eidsfjord side branch meets the main fjord, the seaway to Nordfjordeid, and only a 5km narrow strip of land separates it from a deep lake.

At Nordfjordeid one can turn southwards and eventually reach Bergen by road and ferry, or take the main road northeast towards Trondheim passing Europe's deepest lake, Hornindal Water (*Hornindalvatn*), the 514 metres depth of clear water gives the most beautiful reflections of the trees along the road side and small farms scattered at the base of sheltering hills across the lake on the northern shore. There is hardly a ripple on the water, for no glacial streams flow into it resulting in Europe's cleanest lake. It is not surprising that this peaceful, picturesque area is the home of a few distinctive craftsmen.

On the farmstead at Taraldset I found Rolf with the family name. I was most impressed by his ceremonial chairs, for the carving was done on both sides, back and front, and through the chair-back itself. Here was a sign of the infinite patience of the craftsman's perfection even where it is rarely noticed. I was taught that my embroidery should be as neat on the reverse side as the front until my college lecturer spent a sabbatical year in America in 1948 and returned with the instruction that the dictum no longer applied. The speed of machinery had destroyed the satisfaction of hand production. What a refreshing joy to see Rolf's work, reminiscent of the centuries' old marble lace carving on the Taj Mahal.

Sæter near Loen, on Nordfjord.

Hornindal water (Hornindalvatn) Europe's deepest lake.

Low cloud over Utvik, near Stryn.

I am looking forward to the day when I can take a small road from Nordfjordeid branching off to the right, beside the northern shore of the fjord. You can go a few kilometers along the shore of Utvik until the track becomes a path blocked by steep, mountain rocks protruding into the fjord waterway, which at this point makes a spectacular elbow bend. Hurrah! I have just heard the road is through and the way open, 2008.

The difficulties of road making in Western Norway for vehicular traffic are many, mainly terrain and climate related, and emphasise the age old convenience of natural waterways. 'Vik' appearing in so many names denotes a sheltered creek, a finger-like protrusion of a fjord often hidden from the main stream. It was in such inner creeks that the ancient ships were built, the builders known as 'men of the creeks' - **VIKINGS**.

Nordfjord narrows near Nordfjordeid, separated from lovely Hornindal Water by the mountainous block gouged out by glaciers in times long past. The neck of the fjord here forms a creek, Utvik, which is supplied by two wider creeks each flowing directly, through a lake and river from a glacier, branches of the great Jostedalsbre. This area is Innvik, the inner Nordfjord. It is here we find the renowned tourist centres of Loen, Olden and Stryn. Loen and Olden each developed mainly from one hotel and farm in the mid nineteenth century, easily accessible by ship and yet within the mountains.

I drove for the first time, in August 1975, along a byway from near Stryn, then a village of one short main street, parallel to the mountain river rushing down from the distant Jotunheimen to the fjord. The road gently climbed for a few kilometres, passing a group of buildings, possibly a school, hostel and farms and climbed steeply and suddenly stopped. What a magnificent view!

I did not find this road again until 2002 when I was taken by kind local friends from the now prosperous town of Stryn, along a road that was being opened up. I recognised it as we climbed to a pleasantly prepared view point. There we could stand out above the fjord on the mountain shoulder and gaze, without satellite, over the Nordfjord from the Jostedal Glacier on the left and away into the distant foreground and the deeply set fjord down to the North Sea on the right.

We continued the journey as far as possible, to the mountain barrier, but I had a delightful surprise. We came to a mini-super-market at a tiny village called Hopland on the edge of the fjord with its own

Utvik, Nordfjord towards Olden.

Hopland colonial.

quayside. Do not expect trolleys, queues or cash registers. It does have a shop window, not displaying goods but with a table, chairs and benches! We were welcomed with open arms and immediately given hot coffee from a flask, always ready and local 'coffee cake'. We sat in the shop window and chatted. ('Coffee cake' in Norway does not refer to coffee flavoured / coloured cake but to any cake or biscuit taken with coffee after a meal.)

Eventually I wandered round the shop and it took me back seventy years to the days of my childhood in Yorkshire, England. The shop was dark because most of the wall space was occupied by shelves and the goods displayed were the old familiar names of household goods, grocery, tea, coffee, cocoa, sugar, sweets and chocolate and cleaning materials, needles and thread, pens and pencils and patent medicines. Most of the goods which could not be produced at home were originally imported from foreign colonies like the West Indies. The 'colonials' were allowed to sell wine until 1922 when the state monopoly was established. In the early twentieth century, the yachts brought visitors for the summer, to explore the calm inner reaches of the fjords, the shopping was done at 'the colonial,' not the grocers.'

I have a vivid photograph in my mind of a group of Edwardian gentlefolk taking afternoon tea on the lawn of Faleide Hotel, with a yacht in the background. We passed a derelict building that afternoon in August 2002, and I recognized it – without parasols and sunshades. Faleide had been an important staging post in the earliest days of the Norwegian postal system, the end of a pathway over the mountains to open water and a shipping route. Vehicular traffic could not use the road and modern motorists do not have time for afternoon tea.

The 8 kilometre stretch of road through Hopland to Hennesbygda (route 698) was completed in 2005 at a cost of 27 million Norwegian kroner (approx GBP 2.7m). I look forward to visiting my friends in Stryn and enjoying a new/old view.

Monday, 16th September 2002 found me on the shore of Innvik, in a corner suite of the fourth floor of a very large hotel. It was exactly fifty years since I first visited Norway and this hotel. I had made a point of retracing the route I had made as a young teacher in 1952. I had travelled the length and breadth of the country many times in the intervening years but the unique sight of Scandinavia I had not seen for myself was **the aurora borealis,** the famed Northern Lights.

I had discussed this with learned friends and I even contemplated flying north to Tromsø in December or January but the specialists said even then I could not be certain for there were so many conditions needed to create a display of the spectacular, flashing colours in the dark sky.

After dinner that evening, at exactly 9 p.m. (21.00 hrs) I returned to my room, accompanied by a young English couple who wanted to consult a detailed map I possessed. I unlocked the door and stepped in, expecting to fumble for the light switch but gasped as I found the room flooded with magnificent light through the large balcony windows before me.

"*What is it?*" asked the young banker and his wife. I stared, mesmerised for some moments and moving forward, as though on holy ground, to step onto the balcony, stammered, "*It must be the Northern Lights*". The vision was not the dancing, flashing bands of colour you see in illustrations or on film but a gigantic butterfly, perched between massive mountains, hovering over the Stryn valley at the head of the fjord.

Radiating from the central spiral column of swirling grey and silver, horizontal ribbons of shimmering white, lemon, yellow and gold, stretched wing-like to rest on the distant valley slopes. Above all was an arched, narrow diadem of glittering white and silver light. The fantastic radiance was reflected in the dark saline waters of the fjord and there the iridescence shone in streaks of violet, blue and red.

My camera was ready and set but not a vestige of the breath-takingly brilliant scene was recorded. Pin points of lights along the fjord side were held but the vision itself must have been millions of miles away. I do not want the scientific details of this particular phenomenon. I know that this was a spiritual experience, a vision seared in my soul if not my camera, and I thought of Paul describing such a sight on the road to Damascus to King Agrippa (Acts of the Apostles 26: 12-18) and the shepherds on the hills outside Bethlehem that first Christmas, visited by, 'Angels from the realms of glory…' I never use the word glory, gloriously, or Gloria without giving thanks for my wish fulfilled in God's good time.

Later I have seen the *aurora borealis* on several northern cruises in winter time but never a display this shape and colour. I checked with fishermen in the Lofoten Islands some years later and they confirmed that particular appearance. God comes to us unexpectedly, in unexpected places, at unexpected times. As Bishop of Trondheim from 1758 (inducted 31st July) to his death September 1773, Gunnerus must have seen magnificent displays in the winter months, perhaps better than we see today because they would not be dimmed by pollution, industrial effluence and city lights. A man so closely in tune with nature must have been aware of some message. The subject of astronomy would have been discussed and written about by the three friends, Gunnerus, Gerhard Schøning and Peter Fredrik Suhm - husband of Karen Angell Suhm - meeting in the congenial atmosphere of the Angell family library. It was from the work of this group The Scientific Society developed, and here the seeds for the first university in Trondheim and Norway were planted.

Stryn is now the community centre, no longer a sleepy village but a thriving tourist area including Loen and Olden within its boundary. The coat of arms depicts a golden spray of lind leaves on a green background reminding us that here is to be found the largest copse of linden trees in Northern Europe. The lind, known in parts of Europe as 'lime', is a favourite deciduous Northern Hemisphere tree for its lovely shape and long life.

One renowned 17th century gigantic lind tree was in the family farmyard in Småland, Sweden, and influenced a young man to accept it, in Latinised form, as his surname on his entrance to Lund University. Nils Ingemarssen Linnaeus's son was entered first at Lund University (1727), later Uppsala (1728) as Carl Linnaeus (1707-1778)- the famous **L.** of modern botany. I have gazed with awe many times at the coppice of *Tilia cordata* (lime), estimated to be 2,000 years old, in the Westonbirt Arboretum, Gloucestershire, England, and thought of Linnaeus and his descendant "apostels".

Lind leaves

Nordfjord to Sognefjord

Accompanied by the friendly goldsmith from Stryn, we will take the road through Loen with Innvikfjord on our right-hand side and a few farms and modern dwellings on the left *fjell (fell, hill side)*. I had always known 'fell, dale and foss' in the Yorkshire Dales. We bear left and then right. A local road climbs up to the right, to the white sentinel church with a pleasing view of the inner fjord. The map clearly shows the inmost part of Nordfjord boot-shaped, like Italy. Stryn, like a tag at the back of the boot, leads down to Loen at the tip of 'the heel'. From the church where we pause, the 'instep' conceals 'the toe', Olden, and the coast continues up 'the leg' to the point where we looked across the fjord from Faleide.

The road forward, below the church way, leads up Lodalen beside the short, fast flowing River Lo, to Loenlake (*Loenvatn*) and the great *Jostedalsbreen* (glacier) ahead. The main snout in sight is *Kjenndalsbre* and there are smaller ones at the heads of side valleys, like *Bødalsbre*. It is a picturesque sight with a sombre atmosphere, for the scar on *Ravnfjellet* broods over the scene today.

On Sunday, 13th September 1936 Marie Sunde would have liked to row across the head of Innvikfjorden and up Loen Lake, to visit

Loen Church

Beside Loen Lake looking towards Kjenndalsbre.

her sister at Nesdal and her baby, a few days old, but she was unwell and not fit to journey from home that Sunday afternoon. She herself was heavily pregnant with her second child. The two sisters, born Katrine and Marie Mardal were planning to have their latest offspring baptised at the same time but baby Sunde's late arrival was delaying the christening ceremony (*barnedåp*).

The home farm of Mardal was at the head of the Gloppefjord, near Sandane where the waters of Breim Lake flow gently into the fjord to join the Utvik branch of the Nordfjord, and some kilometres nearer the mouth of the fjord than Stryn on Innvikfjorden. This small property had been inherited by the only Mardal brother, on the early death of the father, and he provided a home for his mother and eked out a living for his own young family by taking in carpentry jobs. The sisters had moved away to nearby areas to gain education, experience and be self-supporting.

Marriage to Mons Nesdal meant Katrine moved into Lodalen to live on part of her husband's family holding, Mons Bruket. There were at least two other Nesdal families in the immediate vicinity indicating typical subsistence farming - sheep, cattle and goats, fresh water fish (small trout are still found in the lake at the foot of the glacier) and, not far away, salt water fish in the fjord. The name, Nesdal, suggests a valley or dale (*dal*) on a narrow spit of fertile land (*ness*).

Meanwhile younger sister, Marie Mardal, had worked in the summer months, before marriage, as a *seter* girl at Bødalseter, across the lake from Nesdal, part of the practical work for her dairying certificate. As a summer tourist guide she chose to wear the Hardangerfjord area national costume of bright red and black with a crisp white apron of open-work embroidery, considering it more attractive than the

Nordfjord one of black and green. Many people abroad still consider the Hardanger dress the Norwegian National costume because of its popular widespread use in the early days of tourism. Marie had taken a one year residential course in domestic science at the ladies' college in Stryn and had further experience in the household of the doctor next door to the college. No wonder the handsome son of the clever, itinerant watchmaker, resident in Stryn, considered her a most suitable wife.

On the fateful Sunday afternoon when disaster struck, Katrine and Mons had five children, Agnes, Olav, Bjarne, Solveig and the tiny unbaptised bairn. They lived in a sheltered, mountain protected valley, blocked at one end by a finger of the Jostedalsbre Glacier but open to the outer world at the other end by a track beside the River Lo.

There was a time at the height of the elite British explorations when ocean going steamers could navigate the river from the fjord to the head of the Lake but that route was abandoned after a rock fall in June 1905. The tidal wave of displaced deep lake water then swept away villages, crushed or drowned 84 and flung the lake steamer, Lodalen, some 250 feet from its mooring, where the rusted wreck can still be seen (2002) though the engine was retrieved and reused.

This tragedy was not enough to relocate persistent farming families from their ancestors' land, from ground that had been laboriously cleared of stones for cultivation, whilst the stones were incorporated in the foundations of their homes and outhouses. Mons Nesdal was of such stock to be found there in 1936 when a great disruption again shattered and swept away homes, villages, families and livestock.

Nesdal farm

Hardanger Bunad in centre.

Loen Lake

Ravnfjell

The steep, east facing boulder strewn scarp of Ravnfjell (The Raven Mountain) cracked, exploded and shattered casting thousands of tons of rock into Loen Lake, pushing the water like a gigantic wave, across the bed of the lake. As it was relentlessly returned by the mountains around Bødal, another farming community across the valley, a further fall occurred in the same place, causing a second flood wave. Homes flooded by the first wave were lifted on the crest of the returning wave, collided with the oncoming surge to be shattered to smithereens in the thunderous crash of uncontrolled, powerful water, two waves meeting hundreds of feet above sea level. In this manner perished Mons and Katrine Nesdal and their five children.

Seventy three names are recorded on the stone tablets standing above the river and fjord before Loen Church, where the recovered earthly remains of a few victims were interred. Poignantly only seventy two names are shown, for under the family name of Nesdal the words, 'unbaptised son', are added - the tiny babe awaiting the arrival of its baby cousin that they might be 'born again in Christ's name,' together.

There is no record of the untold suffering of the few who survived and the relatives and distant friends of the victims. Imagine the anguish of Marie Mardal Sunde when she gave birth to her son three weeks later.

I remember the catastrophe for as a child of six I collected pennies, in a blue silk, draw-string purse made by Miss Wrigglesworth from Sunday School in Yorkshire, to help orphans and homeless in the wild, beautiful distant country of Norway. About the same time at day school we read a story about a little Norwegian boy who got lost in the snow. My teacher, Mrs Jeffries, sent me out of the class room, like a naughty child, because I wept. No one explained why I was 'punished'. It took me sixty years to discover it was a kindness, not a punishment that caused my dismissal. Even then Norway was within my heart or soul, seemingly without rhyme or reason.

There are still occasional rock falls, when the melting ice expands in crevices, but the ancient rock falls embedded in the lake act as a cushion to somewhat deaden the disturbance. No vessel can negotiate the river from the fjord as steamers did a century and a half ago but there is one which plies the lake in summer to within easy walking distance of the glacier and Bødalseter is still in use. Nature has resumed its cloak of green in many places, punctuated with massive stone boulders, impossible to move by manpower but casually flung by the uncontrolled force of ice and the flow of water.

Let us press forward to the glacier, to Kjenndalsbreen. (The pronunciation of this name reminds me of the south-east Asian dessert, *chendol*, consisting mainly of shaved ice). The snout is certainly not as long as when I first saw it 55 years ago. If we could soar over the pale blue crevices of this precipitous face and continue in a south easterly direction, we should fly across the central block of one of the greatest glaciers of Europe, reminiscent of flights over Antarctica. A landfall at the foot of another snout, Nigardsbreen, of the mighty Jostedalsbreen ice cap would be within Jostedalsbreen National Park. Here is a modern Glacial Museum and research station - the movement, recession, condition of the glaciers is being constantly and carefully monitored.

This glacial barrier separated the farming area of the western fjords from the most populous region of Norway around Christiania/Oslo and the access towns and ports to Copenhagen, the Royal seat of

The now 70 year old cousin of the 'unbaptised son' points to the inscription on the memorial stone by the church.

Silt from glacier entering lake.

Loen Lake looking towards Nordfjord.

The old road over to Sogne.

Nigardsbreen

Government and university. In an attempt to provide food as fresh as possible, live cattle were taken once a year from a gathering point in the Stryn area up a valley and over the glacier, along a track known to the most experienced old drovers and eventually down the *Jostedal* valley to Sognefjord. The market was reached by boat and main track.

A few old records of the journeying remain and periodically the route explored. Imagine the cattle owners gathering, deciding how many men could be spared from their own farms and trusted to take their beasts - and return with provisions and money from the big city. Weather conditions were paramount and an attempt would be made to catch the short period at the end of summer whilst the daylight still lasted almost twenty four hours. If it was too warm the ice would be soft and the cattle fall in, or it would refreeze at night so they would slide. The path would deteriorate with the trampling of hundreds of hooves and feet. All food had to be carried with them over the glacier too. It is said that sometimes it was possible to slide animals down the glacier by tying their four legs together and putting them on their side, a personal sleigh!

Once over and into the area of the Sognefjord, there were recognised shelters, where men and beast could rest and regain strength - they must be in good condition when they reached the markets. What joy there would be when they returned home by a longer, but quicker way without cattle and bearing rare provisions on the sledges for the approaching Yuletide (*juletid*), and what stories and experiences of a different world!

One of the old tracks led down my favourite valley in Norway, Jostedal, to the sheltered, mirror like waters of the Lustrafjord, an inner north-easterly branch of the great Sognefjord.

Enough has been written of the longest (some 200km from North Sea coast to Jotunheimen Mountains), deepest (around 1,300m in the area of Høyanger though only 175m deep at the mouth of the fjord) and narrowest (the World Heritage recognised) Nærøy fjord. It is certainly the main sea-artery into the western mountains and includes industrial areas today as well as ancient boat-building yards from viking days.

My affection and interest is held by a once secret valley, the course of the Jostedalselva (*elva* - river), which to my mind is exactly like the River Wharfe in Yorkshire, England. I have known and loved this North Yorkshire river, from its sources on the shoulders of the Pennines to its junction with the River Ouse just south of York and Stamford Bridge, of Viking battle fame (September 1066), all my life.

The river in Jostedal.

When I explored Jostedal for the first time I made very slow progress to the recently opened glacier centre at Nigard. At every bend in the road I caught a glimpse of another childhood scene as the Jostedalselva dashed over limestone rocks like Linton Falls; it sang the same tune as it rushed over the flatter stones like the Ghaistrylls. The steep, grey, scar face across the river began to set the sinister scene, like Loop Scar and the river, now unseen, was pressed into a fast flowing current like the Wharfe at the Strid at Bolton Abbey, deep beneath two massive flat-topped rocks a 'stride' apart.

The small white wooden church in Jostedal was built in 1660. Its compact tower and contrasting black roof gave away no secrets when I rested at its locked gate. The legend tells of the scourge of the Black Death, mid fourteenth century (I think possibly 2 to 3 centuries later), and how a small group of rich merchants escaped from the coastal district into this isolated valley known only by a few farmers

Water worn rocks in Jostedal.

Eyam Church, Derbyshire, England.

A tomb of a victim in Eyam Churchyard who died 25th August 1666.

who may have used the sparse pasture land in summer. The lane was blocked and guards given the command 'Let no one enter' as in Eyam, Derbyshire, England; and especially famed in Oberammergau, Bavaria, in the seventeenth century.

I was curious to see the picturesque 'well dressing' ceremonies again in Derbyshire, England after half a century. It was a popular outing to drive over the Pennines by the Snake Pass and several lake-like reservoirs providing excellent drinking water for developing cities. We could park the car comfortably in a quiet country lane or take 'Afternoon Tea' at some cottage or farmhouse and stroll through a quiet village to view the display beside the well, usually near the church. The 'dress' is a ten to twenty centimetre deep wooden frame, usually about one metre by two metres, mounted on a wooden board. The wooden tray is filled with wet clay and thoroughly soaked in the local river. A biblical or historical illustration is created by inserting individual flower petals into the wet clay. When almost dry and firm the picture can be raised and erected in position, in thanksgiving for the health restoring water of the Derbyshire Dales. Many celebrations take place around St John's or St Peter's day but Eyam's thanksgiving is at the end of August.

It was 3 July 2003 when I returned to Derbyshire. It was impossible to stop a car, except at red traffic lights, masses of people crowded pavements and walkways and I could not even stop to purchase a bakewell tart in Bakewell. I was overcome with remorse on visiting Eyam Church. A dark oppressiveness pervaded the scene and I wanted to escape as quickly as possible. The stark, unending stretch of gravestones, like unproductive stalagmites from flat cold earth, was only alleviated by the green of branching old trees. 'No Parking' signs kept the crowds away.

I longed for the peaceful valleys and the opportunity to contemplate the passing of time, to gain strength to face the future, in tune with the infinite. Was this why the museum keeper near Sogndal said there was no truth in the legend about Jostedal? The historic event has certainly been kept somewhat 'alive' through four centuries in Derbyshire. The same period was even more devastating in a less populated country like Norway changing the course of its history.

In Oberammergau, Bavaria, the Vow was made in 1633, that if God would stop the plague from further decimating the sheltered valley village, the villagers would perform the story of Christ's Passion during every tenth year for ever. This vow is still kept. My sister and I were privileged to share it in 1950 and I know plans are in hand for 2010.

I wonder what effect tourism, commercialisation and particularly technology has had on Oberammergau in sixty years. Numbers of visitors were controlled by the number of seats in the purpose built theatre with a large front stage open to the elements and the natural mountains forming the wings and background. I remember talk of Oberammergau from 1934. My favourite aunt, and treasured godmother, had a flat cardboard box of small silver coins in the upper drawer of her dressing table. She was saving up to go to Oberammergau. That should have been 1940 but there was no performance due to WWII. The saving went on but my auntie had become completely crippled with rheumatoid arthritis (no hip replacements in those days) and sent my sister and I instead. Yes, she should be mentioned here because I consider her a saint and helped me on my early pilgrimage more than any one.

Kilnsey Crag, Wharfedale, Yorks. England.

These are just two illustrations of how traditions have been passed on and history taught but I could not find any firm basis in Jostedal of how some years later people ventured up the dale and found no one, except a flash of black and white, like *a rypa* (white grouse/ ptarmigan), a young, uncouth wild girl. She was taken back to the village and adopted. There remain families in the area who bear names reminiscent of this event and descent from Jostedalsrypa. I met the local historian in 2002 at Kaupanger and was dismissed with, '*No truth in it whatever!*' I am not prepared to accept that as I have been astonished to find some grain of truth in many legends - more details later in our search for Gunnerus.

Some twenty kilometres south down Jostedalen we reach Gaupe and the Lustrafjord. I should pause at Marifjøra, for old times' sake. It is not what it used to be but the glorious beauty of the mirror-like fjord, perfectly reflecting the snow topped mountains around this inner fjord, of an inner fjord of the mighty Sognefjord remains an idyll. Tørvis Hotel was a welcome place of peaceful sojourn, before or after mountaineering, half a century ago. I remember a guest had written,

> '*Lean and thin we staggered in.*
> *Fat and stout we waggled out*'

in the guest book then. Now the hotel was unrecognisable but the smooth, silky waters of the fjord were as lustrous as ever.

Joutunheimen - Home of Gigantic Mountains

We cross the tranquil Lustrafjord by a usually tightly packed ferry. We must admire the accurate agility with which the crew load all the wide variety of vehicles from two-wheeled cycles to trucks and trailers, perhaps carrying a cow. The non-local passengers' attention will quickly have passed over the oddities of cargo to the beautiful building up the hillside from the ferry landing stage. Sitting peacefully and contentedly, on a flat grassy shoulder of the tree covered hill, can be seen the oldest stave church in Norway, parts of it occupying that site since the twelfth century.

At fjord level, down on the right hand side as one climbs to the church, can be seen a small boat yard where vessels are handmade, as they have been here for centuries, for use in this locality. I looked for the type of boat Bishop Gunnerus of Trondheim might have used but these were much smaller and far more fragile than needed in the North of Norway.

URNES is marked on the map *Norges eldste stavkirke (1135AD)* - Norway's oldest stave church. It is fascinating to attempt to date this wooden building. Modern dendrochronologists admit that their present methods cannot exactly place the date of the first building

Urnes, Norway's oldest stave church.

North Portal

of the church. Excavations have revealed there have been two earlier churches on the site, indicated by the position of ground holes where the earliest earth-bound corner posts had been erected. Beneath the oldest site at Urnes Christian graves have been found.

Parts of older wooden churches have been reused in later models making the dendrochronolologists' task more difficult. Here we have the most beautiful carved North Portal, now famous as the classical, typical Urnes style, which may have been the predominant west wall of an earlier church. It is suggested that the carving represents the eternal struggle between good and evil, the four-footed animal at the base, a type of lion symbolic of Christ, wrestling with a twisting, writhing satanic snake. I consider the design may be pre-Christian conversion. The only piece of jewellery I treasure is a gold brooch, a reproduction of grave treasure found in a burial mound of the Viking period (c.1,000AD). It is similar in design to the carving but circular and more complete with its smooth gold twists and turns striving upwards. Many of the early stave churches have highly decorative carved roof-eaves with dragons and mythical creatures, finished as their boat prows, as though they were retaining something of their early gods 'to make sure' they were doing the correct thing although Christianity was being forced upon them by the king and his men.

The external roof beams and eaves of Urnes Church are simply finished but here on the north wall are the graciously engraved panels, reminiscent of the ancient crafts-men's skill and philosophy.

Four solid beams of equal dimension were prepared for the formal foundation of the building; the size would depend on suitable local forests. I can imagine the men choosing the four matching pine trees in autumn and stripping them of branches, making a carpet towards the church site and perhaps being helped by frost and a fall of snow to lubricate the paths as they dragged the sills to the designated positions. There a shallow gravel bed had been prepared and the beams/sills laid on the gravel and notched at the corners to form a rigid ground frame for the building. A vertical beam corner post, with a cross cut bottom, was erected over the joints so making them waterproof.

A groove was then made in the ground sill and trees and branches were split into planks/staves and set upright, packed within the groove from corner-post to corner-post. An upper trimmed wooden plate with a groove below was then fitted over the wall planks and made secure with wooden pegs, wedges and chips. This solid rigid frame with staves formed each side wall of the church and could support the roof rafters and cross beams.

The roof itself consisted of wooden tiles (*takspon*) cleaved from a pine tree of selected diameter cut into circular blocks of the desired height of tiles. The actual tree had been prepared the year before by removing the bark from beneath the crown downwards. In an attempt to seal the wound a special resin was naturally produced providing more resinous timber desirable for roof tiles. Each block was split into segments, the radius giving the width and the depth of block the length, of each tile/*spon*. Experience had taught the woodcraftsmen that splitting the wood in this way, gave natural drainage and more durability than cutting with a saw. The two lower corners of each tile were diagonally cut off leaving a triangular tongue, the apex of which was again acutely trimmed by axe so rain would gently drain. The wooden tile was set to overlap the row of tiles beneath and fastened, in the earliest buildings with wooden pegs, to a wooden batten. Finally the exterior was coated in tar, made locally from the distillation of organic matter such as pine roots and shavings, giving it a weather proofed coat.

Solvorn

Carved corner pillar, Urnes.

47

Walaker, Solvorn

The newest Norwegian Stave Church (2000AD) on Icelandic Westerman Islands.

Over the years the churches developed in size and style. Historians/archaeologists consider there had been between one thousand and two thousand stave churches built in Norway but only 29 remain in the early twenty first century. Standing on the deck of M/S Fram (motor vessel built 2006) I saw the newest stave church to be built, a replica, donated by the Norwegians to the people of the Westerman Islands commemorating the millennium of Christianity in Iceland in the year 2000. I could not see it when we first docked at Heimaey, 7.4km south of the coast of Iceland, Wednesday 24th September 2008. I observed two parallel dark green covered walls with openings opposite each other, set on a grassy shelf at the waters' edge with a black hill background. Could it be a sheepfold? As the sun rose, bit by bit the dark tarred shape of the church became distinguishable, indeed the Good Shepherd's fold.

When I heard of the ancient carving on Urnes Stave Church I was told it was impossible to reach it and it was only an old pile of timber. I persisted and was eventually rowed across the Lustrafjord but not allowed to land. Many, many changes have taken place in Norway during the last half century and treasures have been restored and preserved. Today it is possible to wander round the church yard and view the interior and wonder at the skill of men with primitive tools and patience. Now we can depart by road in a north-easterly direction, without using the ferry, along the shelf-shore of the Lustrafjord towards the mountains before us. At the furthest inland tip of the Sognefjord we join the most northerly highway in Europe and turn to the right along the Sognefjell Road to climb into the Jotunheimen Mountains towards the three highest peaks in Norway.

We take an acute right turn on to Highway 55, on the outskirts of Skjolden. In a few years' time we may be induced to pause in this growing town, the innermost port of the Lustra/Sognefjord, due to be completed as a cruise port mid 2010. Along the shore of Skjolden Lake and the pleasant Fortunsdalen we reach Fortun church. Here the main road turns sharply from the valley and commences its steep climb by hairpin bends to Opptun and along a mountain pass, close between mountains more than 1,000m high, ever upwards to Turtagrø on a small plateau 884m over sea level (Sognefjord). I have paused many times at Turtagrø from the days when it was a staging post for the buses, just a 'toilet stop', to over-night stays in the newest Turtagrø Hotel in August 2007. A few buildings remain from earlier establishments but conflagrations have meant improved accommodations for mountain climbers, hikers, and all who would enjoy the mountainous wonderland of the Jotunheimen block.

The character of Turtagrø changed overnight. We had had a quiet evening in the library enjoying some of the rare writings on mountaineering and viewing trophies and photographs. We had climbed the wooden stairs to our bedroom in the eaves, breathed the fresh mountain air, taken a last distant peep of Sognefjord and slept. We were astonished next morning to come down early to a crowded restaurant. There were a hundred pairs of jaws masticating sandwich after sandwich, a hundred pairs of hands gathering more food around them from a piled serving table, constantly refilled from the ever opening and closing kitchen door. What was happening? Where were all these calories going?

Here, having a last, hopefully fortifying meal, were the seniors and veterans preparing for the annual Turtagrø-Fanaråkan Opp, the Norwegian uphill running championship. Their goal, Fanaråkhytta, poses gracefully 2,068m above sea level, a southern bastion of the 'giants'. (A *jotun* was a mythological giant thought to live inside a mountain

Turtagrø 2002.

Anxiously watching the cloud on Fånaråkan and awaiting the returning race participants. 2007

Turtagrø

Sognefjell road.

Sognefjell

*The Horungtinder
from the Suletind*

*After the water colour drawing
by the late Mr James Backhouse*

and constantly at war with gods and men and, not surprisingly, *heim* means home). Some of the helpers and supporters remained on the steps of Turtagrø Hotel watching the cloud movements over Farnaråken during mid-day and for the return of medallion carriers.

We resumed our journey eastward on this occasion across the Sognefjell Plateau pausing many times to just gaze at the stark panorama, to admire the tarns reflecting glacier or cloud and the mountains range after range. I stopped. Memories flooded back. Like the journey down Jostedal there was something familiarly homely to me. I thought of William Cecil Slingsby (1849 - 1929), the Yorkshire man from Craven near Skipton who was one of the first men to climb the highest of these peaks. He is still considered '*the father of mountaineering*', as a sport rather than a necessity. His book, '*Norway, the Northern Playground*' published officially in 1904 has recently been republished and still has some insight to offer climbers today. I know where an original copy of the book resides - very special, for it has a dedication in Slingsby's own writing to Greenwood, his personal friend who provided many sketches in the book. Then too there were Kilnsey Crags, Malham Tarns, Pen-y-ghent ...

I turned once more to geology, of what were these rocks formed? I was always told in Wharfedale, 'limestone' and looked for the minute sea shell remains. Now my search, through modern methods, brought me intense joy and satisfaction. I discovered that Geography was enhanced in schools by Earth Science; that orogeny, the genesis

This sketch by Eric Greenwood (initials sketched lower right hand) of the Hurangtinder mountains in this region is from Slingsby's "Norway" actually copied from Greenwoods book, a Christmas present from Slingsby, 1903. It was based on a water colour by James Backhouse, another Yorkshire botanist, and relative of E. Backhouse mentioned later.

of mountains through the movement of plate tectonics, had over millions of years slowly provided the eruptions of mountain chains. These mountain ranges have been sculptured, axed and ground by ice, wind, storm and fire over centuries so revealing some of the innermost core of the earth. My inner being rejoiced to find that the Pennines of Yorkshire (the backbone of England), the Highlands of Scotland (I had always known the lochs and NW Highlands as 'poor man's Norway') were part of the same structure as the mountains of Norway, the Caledonian Orogeny. This too explains my innate love of Norwegian botany, very similar to the flowers I had known in the Yorkshire dales from childhood.

Poles mark the edge of the Sognefjell Road and indicate depth of snow when road is closed.

Returning to the Sognefjell Road we descend from Krossbu in a deep valley, beside a swift flowing stream, and cross into the broader Leirdalen. The mountain road from Jotunheimen Fjellestue to Opptun is usually closed to traffic from the beginning of September until June by snow. It is traditional that all available local people start from Bøvertun and from Fortun/Opptun on 1st June to open the way again. In Leirdalen we must stop to see Norway's highest mountain, Galdhøpiggen regally standing 2,468m above sea level beyond a lovely valley on the right. Yes, I have climbed to the top of Galdhøpiggen, roped across the glacier as we went up from Juvasshytta, but that wasn't yesterday! Much more exciting, we have a friend, now ninety years old, who was married on the top of Galdhøpiggen in 1944. The ceremony was performed very quietly and secretly in occupied Norway and even Per Prest (Rev Sæther) and a few very close friends, climbed with them. Imagine a bride in hob-nailed boots and corduroy knee-britches hitch-hiking from Lillehammer, part way to the Jotunheimen, on a local brewery dray! Tulla could not wear a traditional golden bridal crown in those difficult days but she did have a beautiful crown of local wild flowers.

Galdhøpiggen 2,468 m.

Specimen of mountain flora, from Galdhø-piggen 2008.

Jotunheimen

Down over Galdhøpiggen.
Water colour by William Heaton-Cooper

Lom commune

Leirdalen leads us into Bøverdalen and passing Elvesæter and Røisheim we reach Lom, 83km from Skjolden, on the western coast over the roof of Norway to the great eastern valleys. Fifty years ago Lom was just a church and a bus stop. I can remember using the lovely old stave church as a bus shelter in the rain when we had some time to wait for our next bus connection. It was my first introduction to a stave church and I must say my waiting time was well spent. Today Lom is a thriving town, a community centre with a fascinating coat of arms for an inland valley township, depicting three spades, like oars, on a blue background. It is a natural focal point where the River Bøvra from the heights of Sognefjell flows into the extensive Otta River, wide enough in places to be called a lake, as Ottavatn and Vågåvatn, before it reaches the town of Otta. There the icy green waters of the River Otta flow beside the blue waters from Dovrefjell and gradually merge with the mighty River Lågen to eventually escape into the Skagerrak.

Lom Kommune, although settled round a T-valley junction, where the high powered river Bovra dashes into the broader Otta River, at an approximate angle of 90 degrees, is 382m above sea level and is surrounded by one of the driest areas in Norway. It is said to be as dry as the Sahara Desert in Africa. The average annual temperature ranges from -10°C in January to 14°C in July (sunny summer periods can range from 14°C to 26°C) The surrounding high mountains, over 2,000m above sea level, may have snow falls any time of year. The average rainfall is given as 321mm (12.6ins) per year but strangely enough throughout the summer season, wet or fine, you will notice many crops receive a constant spray of water, automatically pumped and spread. This is because the soil is particularly fertile and the long summer daylight is particularly fruitful-we look forward to the almond shaped potatoes with their thin skin and smooth sweet flesh.

Glittertind

Irrigation has gone on in this part of the country for centuries. It has been gradually developed from the seventeenth century when wooden channels were laid from the perpetual snow fields down to the valley farms. The melting snow could be directed where needed by blocking the stream, diverting it into a scraped, or even foot made channel, between the crops. The farmer then walked down the channel using his wooden spade or paddle, scooped up the water and flung it to left and right so spraying his crops like rain. He then removed the stoppage and placed it further down his field. Dams were built where convenient and later canals cut. You will now understand the three spades on the coat of arms which brought water-giving life and prosperity to this dry area. (There was an old adage in Lom which prayed, '*If God would provide the sunshine man would provide the rain*'.)

The cyclical aquatic system had been naturally absorbed and enhanced over the centuries. There were no massive concrete dam

Fjord-Finn our mountain guide.

Delicate mauve tettegrass growing on the bank of an irrigation canal.

Stage 1.

Stage 2. Fresh milk on tettegrass. 7 days later thickening is evident.

walls to dominate the scene, no pump shafts disturbing the quietness. We may have seen two other vehicles that beautiful day in July, 2005 when we turned off the main road from Otta, just before Lom, near Brimi the gastronomical centre of this part of Norway, and climbed a gated road upwards away from the roar of Harley Davidsons and the retardation of carahomes.

FjordFinn, our modern mountaineering expert, knew the way and led us gently to the shoulder of Glittertind (2,464m), the mountain second only to Galdhøpiggen (2,468m) in height in Norway, through lush agricultural land in Meadalen. We paused at Sålell and shared a path beside a banked up canal with a cow. Further into the green, marshy mountains we stopped to admire the view towards the ice field and Glittertind. I opened the car door and beside the lane I caught a delicate flash of amethyst in the damp grass. It could not possibly be my favourite shy violet at this time of year or in this open place! I knelt down to examine the plant and when my eye travelled down to the rosette of leaves at the base of the stem I suddenly realised it was the very plant I had been searching for all summer and had only previously seen pictures.

Enjoying yoghurt with our cereal one morning the question suddenly arose, how was yoghurt made? We quickly found it was first made in Turkey, milk curdled by bacteria but what bacteria? These questions led to enquiries amongst Norwegian friends as to how *tjukkmjølk*, the local thickened milk used to be made. What started the beginning? Some people vaguely remembered having it in childhood, especially those who had grandmothers with summer farms in the eastern valleys, and eventually we found the starting ingredient was a wild flower called *tettegras*. When the women and girls left the home farm in summer to attend to the seter, the men were so occupied they did not have time to regularly attend to the few cattle left for their personal requirements. A few pieces of *tettegras* were placed in the bottom of a milk churn and daily remainders were simply added. In time the milk thickened and some could be used to start a further supply in much the same way as a little dough was retained as yeast for the next baking day.

What was it about the species that did the trick? We must find out for ourselves for even TINE would not, or could not, answer our queries. First we had to find the flower and as local enquiries from likely sources were unsuccessful I turned to the botanists, found its Latin name, *Pinguicula vulgaris* and an illustration and so began the search. You can imagine the thrill of recognition that day as we turned left towards Smådalen with streams of water from Trollsteinhøin, and Glittertind before us.Once we had identified the plant we found masses of is amongst the stones and grass in the damp land near the dams.

A thin, elegant reddish brown stem, 7 to 18cm long , with very fine glandular hairs which cannot be seen without careful inspection, grows from the centre of a tightly packed, basal rosette of ovoid shaped pointed leaves. Flowering in June/July the delicate tiny, blue-mauve flower has an elongated throat, like a minute spur which helps to balance it on the fragile stem. The important part of the plant is at the base of the stem. The yellow, green leaves are from 2 to 5cm long with one central vein and the edges curl over revealing the very pale underside. Here is the secret! The leaves exude a sticky, oily liquid which attracts tiny insects. They stick to the leaves, the edges of which gently roll over them trapping, suffocating and digesting them. *Tettegras* is one of the two carnivorous species to be found in Norway. It is the insects in the leaves that curdle and thicken the cream.

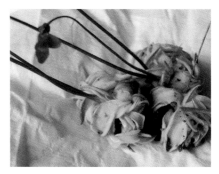

Clearly shows insects stricking to leaves and the edges of the leaves rolling over to trap and suffocate them.

The 'sæterboy' now!

The water-shed between Geirangerfjord and Nordfjord.

We now had the basic ingredient. Having taken the advice of the wife of the world famous plant hunter, Roy Lancaster, we had a plastic shower-cap tucked away in a pocket corner for use as a modern vasculum and could transport a plant for 'scientific research' back to base.

The second stage in our production of tettemilk proved a further modern difficulty. We failed once or twice but then found the milk would only curdle if we used whole fresh milk, straight from the cow. This was difficult to obtain in our modern dairying system but one Sunday kind friends in Lesja came to our aid and within a few days our experiment proved successful. We were fortunate too to have the help and guidance of a medical doctor friend who had been a *seter* boy on his grandmother's farm in his distant youth in Røros in the Glomma valley.

Still looking for traces of Bishop Gunnerus, the collector of the first *Flora Norvegica*, I naturally investigated this publication of 1766 onwards, which rests in the Horticultural Library of the Warwickshire College, Leamington Spa, England. This is the book which set me off on my botanical pilgrimage of Norway in the twenty first century. Interestingly it was there demonstrating how clergy in his bishopric of the north had collected local knowledge. In this entry he reports it flowering in Evenes on 9 June 1767 and on the island of Loppa and in West Finmark and we know from Gunnerus' own records that he was there in 1767 on his third journey to the far north of his diocese acccompanied by Jacob von der Lippe Parelius, who was later to take charge of the Scientific Society's collection and their Danish friend, Professor Oeder, who included *Pinguicula vulgaris L* in his famous collection, '*Flora Danica*'. (The letter L after a name indicates it was first described by Linnaeus). Gunnerus also gives the English name of the plant, Butterwort.

I found butterwort had been profusely used in England too in the 17th - 18th centuries for much the same purposes as in Norway - its very name 'butterwort' refers to the thickening process in the making of butter. James Sowerby writing around 1790 records the use of the greasy, oily substance produced on the leaves in Yorkshire as a soothing ointment for the delicate parts of cows. The plant is found throughout the northern hemisphere especially in countries which have cold winters.

It was with exhilaration we left this fantastic area - so much so, I could swing on the five barred gate as I opened and closed it for our exit to the present world, as I was taught to do almost eighty years ago, but there was no 'penny' for me now! There was something more valuable. Ancient and modern were found harmoniously together creating a peaceful, paradise in a crowded, busy world.

We took the main road back to Lom and followed the old trading route up Ottadalen to Grotli. The old road branches off to the left here and is always closed in winter but it finds new life often in summer as a summer ski resort. I have travelled this way in August, down to Stryn along a road cut through a metre of snow - my Danish driver was so fascinated by the snow he did not want to move down through Videseter to the valley below. We shall keep to the upper road, which is joined by a tunnelled road from Nordfjord today, and turn right to Djupvasshytte and the watershed between the Nordfjord and the Romsdalfjord and the meeting point of the three county boundaries of Oppland, Sogn & Fjordane and Møre & Romsdal.

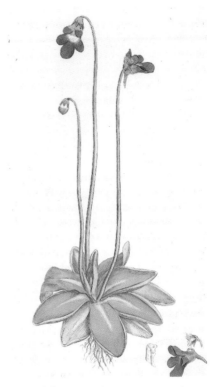

Original illustration from James Sowerby's "English Botany" published in England, in parts, from 1790. The hand coloured print perfectly shows the shape of the flower and leaves but does not indicate the important activity of the leaves – the trapping of the bacteria. Perhaps this was only discovered later.

Pinguicula vulgaris
Butterwort (English)
Tettegras (Norwegian)

GEIRANGERFJORD *c. 1900. Water colour by Alfred Heaton Cooper*

The Moat Round the Western Mountain Block - Storfjorden and Romsdalsfjorden

We descend from the barren rocky plateau, dotted with tarns and often ice and snow covered, along route 63. At present this stretch of road between Grotli and Djupvasshytte is closed from September until June each year by snow and rock falls but constant engineering work is in hand to remedy the situation. The winter blockage means farms and villages, especially those a distance from fjords, may be cut off for several months. Every effort has been made in Norway over recent decades to make permanent open ways to all towns and villages - beautiful bridges have joined islands to the mainland replacing aged ferries; tunnels have been cut through mountain rocks to shelter and protect roads; the work continues.

I think, particularly on this road, we should pause and remember the architects, civil engineers, local farmers, their ancestors and descendants, pilgrims and travellers who have provided these hazardous routes, by footwork, digging, chipping, chopping and carrying over centuries. We have climbed up the old track from Geiranger to Vesterås and imagined the pack horses and merchants seven centuries ago, clambering and sliding over rocks and through mud to carry dried fish, herrings, iron, salt and fabrics over to Lom and the eastern valleys in exchange for pitch or tar for the preservation

The divide between Romsdalfjord and Nordfjord.

The upper road from Djupvasshytta towards Geiranger.

The road snakes its way from the centre-right of the picture down to the head of Geirangerfjord.

of their boats and homes, birch-bark, leather, live falcons and other merchandise. The pack-horse train would serve the coastal area by fjord craft and then overland from the Geirangerfjord.

The outer world began to open when the first steamship, D/S Søndmøre, sailed up Geirangerfjord in 1858. There was one farm at the head of the fjord owned by the Merok family and the quayside was marked on maps until quite recently as Merok - the fjord itself was always Geirangerfjord. There was only one shop on the quayside on my visits in the nineteen fifties and sixties and that was Merok's. I still have little cardboard boxes marked 'Merok' which contained enamelled spoons or brooches purchased there. It was the highlight of the holiday, after a hard day's climb, to gloat over the show cases at Meroks' before the then easy climb (arduous now) back to Union Hotel beside the noisy waterfall. In 1952 Mrs Hans Mjelva had a tiny shop on the bend across the road. Now, if it is still there, it just protects the massive rock on which we celebrated St Hans, midsummer's eve bonfire 1963 to welcome the return of the sun.

The first known foreign tourist yacht to visit Geiranger was the 'Nereid' (Greek name for Sea-nymph), owned by Mr Edward Backhouse (1808-1879) of Darlington, in the summer of 1869. It was a luxurious vessel and I regret I cannot reproduce my copies of Edward's photographs here but they were accidentally destroyed by fire/water in March 2008. (Originals safely in the archives of Sunderland Public Library). Edward Backhouse was born into a wealthy banking family which had been closely associated with the Quaker movement from its foundation in Lancashire in 1652. His interest in Norway had been roused by an uncle, William (1779 - 1844), who had connections with some Quakers from Stavanger. Edward, a bank director and amateur artist, was to accompany William in 1844 but a few days before the departure

date William stood to minister at the Darlington Quaker Meeting and dropped dead. The funeral was on the day they had been due to sail. The ship he was due to have travelled on foundered crossing the North Sea and all lives were lost. Edward accepted this as a God given sign and from then on dedicated his life and artistic talents to ministering God's word.

A monolithic stone moved in the road-making now in the geologic park.

Edward Backhouse 1808–1879. Following the death of a close botanist friend with whom Edward had visited Stavanger, his health broke down and the stress of his responsibilities demanded he withdraw and seek the quiet, strengthening peace of Norway. Staying first in the Stavanger area, using 'Nereid' as base, Edward designed the Quaker Meeting House in Hospitalsgaten 12, Stavanger in 1869. He took the first known photograph of Lysefjord and from the photographs available in his personal album it would seem they cruised northwards and turned into the Storfjord and its inner reaches including Geirangerfjord. Edward Backhouse himself declared, 'a visit to Norway restored him'. Long may its restorative powers remain!

Geiranger was becoming accessible to a few mountaineering tourists. The first guest house, the farm of Martinus K. Merok, was opened near the quayside in 1867, as a necessity, for the local council had decided that the fifteenth century riding track should be improved. A director of Norwegian Public Roads Administration eventually became personally involved. Director Hans Hagerup Krag, (1829-1902) the joint founder of the Norwegian Mountain

Dynamite for the road making was stored behind this waterfall (Geologic Park).

Fifteenth century track.

The Knot completed in 1882.
(Photo Arne Aasheim)

Touring Association in 1868, was the driving force in this project and frequently stayed at Merok's Guest House, possibly the first guest. The wheels of progress turned very slowly in the nineteenth century and it was not until 1877, after legislation and funding had been gradually granted by the local authority and the Storting, that the road could be redefined and marked. The traffic count in 1879 showed that 300 travellers and 30 tourists used the way over the mountains to Lom during the summer. Rosenqvist, the far sighted clerk of works, declared that this spectacular road, once the natural objects were surmounted, would become the country's most important tourist route.

Visitors came to view the stupendous mountains from the smooth comfort of a ship on the reflective waters of the fjord but some were curious and desired to search the hidden valleys and climb the rocky heights. The local farmers found they could earn a little extra money by conveying one or two passengers a distance up the mountain in the light carriage the family used, to some view point, like Flydal. Krag proposed in 1880 that a road should be built to Dalsnibba to enhance the tourist prospect and he worked hard to further the road making. Not all ideas were successful. There were many difficulties to face, seasonal change, movement of rocks and levelling of terrain but the most difficult task was surmounting a mountain crag. Work started at Hole, 29 November 1881, and the following year saw the completion of the elegant, ingenious feature, known as the Knot. Under foreman Ole Knudsen Moen the civil engineers had twisted the road over itself, like a knotted rope, creating the first 'intersection' in the country. 'The Knot' is still usable, though not advisable. The photograph shows us at 'the Knot' in the celebratory procession of the Geiranger collection of vintage cars on the day Geiranger was placed on the prestigious list of World Heritage Sites, 15 July 2005.

'The Flag was high' that clear, sunny day with the QE II anchored in the fjord and the first tourist ship to greet the news.

Excitement must have been high on 15 August 1889 when a four wheeled carriage drawn by two horses arrived in Geiranger from Lillehammer following the final inspection of the completed road. The carriage returned to Lillehammer the next day. There had been at least one previous celebration on sectional completion, as on 14 September 1887, when a stretch of 21km to the county boundary was finished after six years of hard labour, much by local men - and women too who had no doubt fed and supported them in their arduous task, all work done with muscular strength.

Farm above Geiranger showing the 'drive-in' hayloft above the cowsheds and stables.

Krag's pioneering project in promoting tourism in Geiranger was certainly significant though it was not until 1939 that the private four kilometre gravel road was opened for buses leading up to 1,476m summit of Dalsnibba. I remember my first trip up, in a rickety small bus, in August 1957. The matron of our local maternity hospital, sitting beside me, declared '*Oh! This would be wonderful scenery to die in!*' I think I had my eyes closed frequently as we were swung round another hairpin bend and almost over the outer edge of the precipitous road. But it was worth it! The bird's eye view clearly shows how the fjord got its name, the spear head cleft into the steep mountains making a narrow water channel - **geir** - a spear and **anger** - an old word for fjord. Today, especially since the secret was released to World Heritage, we may attain the height in comfort and view the surroundings as 140,000 cars did in 2005. Perhaps you would enjoy the gruelling cross country cycle race from the Geiranger fjord to the summit of Dalsnibba, (climb of 1,500m, 35 180-degree bends and 1 270-degree twist at 'The Knot', **Knuten**) and a free coach ride back to the fjord for cyclist and cycle from the summit.

Geirangerfjord from Dalsnibba.

The Knot. (Photo Peder Otto Dybvik)

Dalsnibba cycle race 2005.

Krag and Rosenqvist had certainly seen the unique attraction of this jewelled stretch of water enveloped by fascinating, snow-capped mountains, flushed with waterfalls, sometimes graceful veils and other times raging torrents, and all almost concealed from the developing world. The visitors came, some to examine and wonder at the feats of engineering whilst others were held by the revelation of nature. Their needs were catered for by the development of hotels and motorised vehicular traffic.

One location in the village which has remained unchanged through many ages, determined by nature and accessibility, is the idyllic church set on a hill-side shoulder above the quayside. The first mention of a church in Geiranger is to be found in 'Trondhjems Reformsats' from 1589 though it is considered there had been a church on the site from around 1450. It must have been on the fringe of the Bishopric of Trondheim to be included in this sixteenth century survey following the Reformation of the Church. (It is interesting to note seats were added after the Reformation, previously standing room only').

The church was demolished in 1742 and a new wooden cross church, with 'rosemaling' interior paintings (local artistry) built in 1744. Johan Ernst Gunnerus became Bishop of Trondheim, appointed by King Fredrik V (1723-1766) of Denmark-Norway in 1758 and I have found no mention of Geiranger in his journal or protocol. We do find however, his colleague and friend, Hans Strøm, quoted in 'Geiranger kyrkje 150 år 1842-1992' booklet that Geiranger chapel, an annex of Sunnylven Church at the head of Sunnylvsfjord, had little land and gave less duty in fish to the bishopric. It was a controversial matter in the latter part of the eighteenth century whether the churches on the south side of Storfjord were in the Bishopric of Bjørgvin (now Bergen) or Nidaros (now Trondheim) and it has only been settled in recent decades by the creation of the Bishopric of Møre og Romsdal with the Bishop's Seat in Molde, the main town on the Romsdalsfjord. But we do know that on 5th September 1773 Bishop Gunnerus of Trondheim preached in Molde and Hans Strøm joined his party. A few days later he had to deputise at Kvernes for the bishop who had been taken ill. Strøm remained with his friends some days. Gunnerus died peacefully in the early morning of Saturday 25th September 1773, but where did he die? This is what I am searching for. I am sure Hans Strøm would know.

I love to stand in the precincts of the white painted octagonal Geiranger Church and look out over the fjord. As I watch a tiny, white speck rounds the grey shadowy 'pulpit rock'. It becomes larger as it approaches the quay-side, cutting a clear victorious wedge through the still, Sunday morning fjord and leaving streams of silver behind. Stepping ashore, the pilot anchors his white ship, picks up his cassock and brief-case and the village priest mounts the road to the church. Pastor Runde reminds me of the Bishop of Trondheim who visited his flock so frequently, near and far, by ship. During the week, I feel guilty using the common path through the churchyard to the quayside, for I remember how Jesus condemned the people taking a short cut through the Temple courtyard in Jerusalem.

The picture of Geiranger church my mind holds dearest was seen early one dark December morning. There had been more snowfall in the night and as I looked from my bedroom window I could see a snow plough cutting its zigzag way down the side of the mountain along the road from Eidsdal. The vehicle headlight could be seen faintly as it moved towards a hairpin bend, but as it turned direction the light shone a strong, straight beam across some five kilometres

Geiranger – a winter idyl!

Pastor Runde approaches.

One of the Geiranger fleet of vintage cars.

Geirangerfjord hesd from Dalsnibba.

Fjordsenter on left, Union Hotel on right and Geirangerfjord in background.

of darkness, directly to the top of the church steeple. I watched this procedure fascinated, as the church was illuminated so precisely at each turn of the road as the snow plough worked its way gradually down the hill.

I have taken an interest in the building of the Eagles' Road since August 1952 when I walked along the road beside the fjord and climbed to the first bend which was being completed. The road was finished in 1955. In 1957 my mother and I, and five retired professional ladies, were able to go by bus up the Eagles' Road (there had been a suggestion that there had been an eagles' nest amongst the crags at the bend which gave the best view of the fjord). We gradually descended Eidsdale to the Valldal ferry, crossed Norddalsfjord and faced another climb.

If you stop today at the view point on the Eagles' Road you will find a safe, railed rock platform which provides stupendous views. There is some surfaced parking but I cannot promise you space at this spectacular spot these days, for during the season it is crowded with 'quick snap' coach tourists. If you would see heaven on earth, have time to stop and take in its glory, choose your time of day and season. Looking straight ahead from the Geirangerfjord, raise your eyes slowly to the right along the steep mountain walls of the fjord and you will glimpse magnificent waterfalls (occasionally catch a rainbow) and see an old shelf farm like Knivsflå near the Seven Sisters Foss.

Your attention may have been captured by the range upon range of mountains before you but turn and look to the left hand side. There, beyond the cruise ships, you see the small town centre of Geiranger gathered tightly round an enlarged quay, the church half-way up the hill and the expanding, residential 'top shelf' of

Geiranger. There, like a gigantic spear stuck into the mountain side is the modern Geirangerfjord World Heritage Centre set on an area of flat ground, stretching to a gurgling stream gathering power as it reaches the old, original, small power station before dashing down to the fjord, and here are plenty of parking spaces. Within the building is something for everyone. You may experience for yourself in a few minutes, with all five senses, how hard working men, women and children cultivated and preserved this almost secret paradise of Northern Europe whilst wrestling a living from a country only 3% of which could be productive. From a collection of exhibits and material brought together by the State Roads Authority for the Centenary of the Geiranger Road in 1989 evolved the Fjordsenter and assisted in World Heritage recognition for Geirangerfjord in 2005.

Icides beside the road to Eidsdal.

Road work continues. On my visits to Norway in the nineteen fifties and early sixties I always wore out two pairs of shoes, soles and heels, on the gravel roads which had to be remade every spring. My first walking shoes in 1950 were a pair of boys' shoes with commando soles and they took some breaking in on the Yorkshire fells. Fashions and needs change - what wonderful, comfortable equipment is available today to suit every terrain and climate.

Tafjord

We can pass from Geirangerfjord overland to Norddalsfjord, another inner branch of Storfjord ending with Tafjord, and after a convenient ferry, travel northwards overland to Romsdalsfjord. A short detour can be made just before taking the ferry, towards Norddal Church and there turning right up the valley and bearing left you will have the peak of Herdalseter before you. Here, in summer you will find Åshild and her *seter* girls tending the flock of goats and preparing cheese and traditional delicious *seter* foods for your delight.

Herdalseter girls.

Herdalseter

Barren plateau above Romsdal.

Stigfossen

Route 63 climbs gently up a winding valley, Valldalen, through acres of strawberry beds. Go in summer time and you will find crowds of students and foreign workers colourfully working their back-aching way over black polythene sheets to gather the most delicious strawberries available. The long daylight hours of Norwegian summertime and the fresh, clear water from the mountains produce these fine crops. (Cream is readily available from the *seter*). By the time you have eaten your strawberries and spent half an hour passing through dreary rocky barren country there is a sudden change. There are a few large picnic spots and crowds of people and buses and nothing beyond them! So it seems, until you reach the edge of the plateau and gaze over. Some three hundred and twenty meters below your feet is the green fertile valley of Isterdalen broadening out until you can spy in the far distance the glittering waters of Romsdalsfjord and the town of Åndalsnes.

We reach the valley by means of another civil engineering feat, *Trollstigveien* (literally 'the Trolls' path), a most impressive way opened 21st July 1936 by King Haakon VII (1872-1957). We could repeat the details of the Geiranger Road engineering but I do not think it necessary, suffice to say there are 11 bends (I think more acute than Dalsnibba), it took 8 years to construct, has a 9% incline and is usually open to traffic from the end of May to early October. Stigfossen, the waterfall, which has worked on the mountains millions of years to form this deep cleft, is 320m in height. The road is so narrow and deep that we cannot appreciate the mountains we travel beneath - they are much more exciting from a distance. Unfortunately for me we cannot stop and examine the tiny gems of nature which must be near our feet but 'eyes open' and we will soon find more elsewhere.

Eighteen kilometres down Isterdalen we meet E136, a main artery from Åndalsnes to Dombås en route for Trondheim or Oslo. Here we have a classical, picturesque transport trio, railway, road and River Rauma running happily side by side for most of the way in Romsdalen parallel with the procession of sharp peaks of the Trollveggen Wall hedging them in on one side and curving round the distinctive Romsdals Horn and Vengetindane on the other. At Fossbru the railway crosses the road and river and after pausing on the bridge over Vermafoss it makes a wide semi circular turn, crossing road and river on the Kylling Bridge, creeps through a short tunnel to Plassen and continues 3km back down the other side of the valley to Fossberget. Here the track loops completely round in the Stavernstunnelen cutting deeply into the mountain to retain a suitable gradient and emerges in daylight some 60m above the previous section, 200m above the road and river. Across the valley from Verma station is Vermadalen and the famous hydro-electric power station well supplied by lakes and streams from mountains like Vermatinden (1477m) and Døntinden (1664m) (*tinden* - the peak).

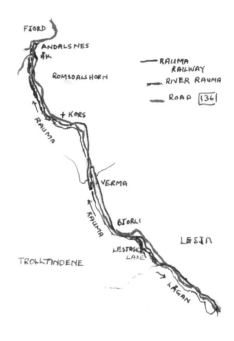

The railway continues, crossing once more the road and river near the county boundaries of Møre og Romsdal and Oppland at Stuguflåten. The Rauma Railway was opened in 1924 but the quiet, narrow Romsdal area had a secret moment of notoriety in 1906 when King Haakon VII and Queen Maude (1869-1938) were on the way to their coronation in Trondheim. They had traversed Gudbrandsdalen from Lake Mjøsa to Otta by train and proceeded to Veblungsnæs / Åndalsnes by horse drawn carriages. The King, the first monarch of the independent Kingdom of Norway for some five hundred years was determined to make a good impression on the people who had chosen him. To demonstrate his awareness of local issues and attention to detail, the director of the procession and driver of the first carriage, Mr Johan Iversen of Lillehammer, was told to quietly stop at a suitable remote position on this road. The attendant guards provided a quick provisional discreet screen with blankets and the king changed from

The valley of the River Rauma.

River Rauma

The jagged mountain peaks of Trollveggen and Trolltindane.

Romsdalshorn from Vengedalen.

the uniform of General to the uniform of Admiral. He greeted his navy on ds Heimdal as Admiral of the Fleet and continued his journey from Åndalsnes to Trondheim. This incident was reported by Mr Iversen to my amanuensis and later confirmed by the driver of the second carriage, Mr Roverud, who carried the Lady in Waiting with the infant Prince Olav.

Hounded by the German invaders in May 1940, the King and his cabinet, appointed to act on behalf of the Storting, hurriedly paused at Stuguflåten, then on the railway line from Dombås to Åndalsnes. Originally a farm village Åndalsnes had developed into a shipping town for the convenience of the railway, so avoiding the necessity of further bridges over the widening mouth of the Rauma - Istra rivers with bends and ox-bow lakes. All Norwegian shipping, world wide beyond occupied Norway (1002 ships), was commandeered to form a national company, Nortraship, for the duration of the war. Surviving vessels were returned to private ownership at the conclusion of hostilities.

Returning down Romsdalen from the watershed of Bjorli - perhaps I should have said 'snow shed' for it is well known for its long winters of heavy snow fall, the mountain heights block the precipitation from the wet, warm, westerly winds from the Atlantic Gulf Stream, creating the dry region of Lesja further beyond to the east. At times a tunnel has to be cut through the snow to the waiting train at Bjorli and a couple of winters ago snow had to be exported to Lillehammer for the World Ski Mastership in March. We will travel at midsummer after taking a typical summer festive meal in Bjorli. The area is well-known for the preparation of *seter* foods and we enjoyed *spekemat* (thinly sliced meats and sausages, salted, dried and preserved), *rømmegraut* (sour cream porridge) and local strawberries and cream, before we set off down the valley in June, 2008.

The outstanding feature of this dale is the rock massif of the Romsdalshorn. The peak is clearly shown on the maps as being 1,550m high but the locals insist it is 1,555m. It was first climbed in 1827 by two Norwegians, Hans Bjermeland and Christen Hoel (Slingsby calls him a blacksmith, Kristen Smed – Kristen is near enough and Smed means blacksmith but he gives the date as 1832!) taking up a dare during a merry making festive party at Veblungsnes. They reached the top by alternately pushing and pulling, built a cairn but were too afraid to come down for two days when hunger became imperative. It was a more difficult task to blindly find foot-holds on the sheer rock face than to stretch up for visible hand-holds. The local mountaineer, A. R. Heen, checked later and certainly found the cairn. I am told it is still in place and can be seen from Aak. From Vengjedalen, the summit appears like the buttress of a great cathedral nave supporting a high spire.

I should like to leave out mention of Aak, to keep it a secret, but that would be being selfish. It took many years to find and even more to get inside. I had read of Aak hotel as the oldest guest house in Norway used by foreign visitors, the haunt of fishermen. I had searched for it several times and it had been suggested that it had burnt down. On reading Slingsby's classic, 'Norway: The Northern Playground' published in 1904, I determined to make a further search in 2004. The first Norwegian who befriended me around 1955 had now become my companion and willing to bring his knowledge, experience and interests to my aid. Our young friend, Fjord Finn, spotted a sign on his homeward way, on a rather difficult bend on the road, so called in on his return. He arranged to take us but we could only get in two nights between conferences. This was a waft of heaven!

On a later occasion we explored, or rediscovered, the delights of the area with a small group of friends forming a house-party. From the

Romsdalshorn from Aak.

Our favourite picture of Romsdalshorn, Aak and Rauma, painted in 1814. Artist unknown.

Looking towards Isfjord from Vengedalen.

Happy group in Vengedal 2008.

Dombås Railway Station where entrance and exit are via tunnel.

moment of entry you are taken back to the time of the old farm with its ladder-like spiral staircase to the upper floor (original loft), to a rock faced wall decorated with climbing equipment and I am sure there would be fishing tackle about. An old treadle sewing machine not only reminded me of childhood homes but indicated the clothing industry which developed in this area, done in piece work in many homes.

I believe Aak had originally been a much larger farm some centuries – the portion stretching down to the river being cut off by the making of a permanent highway at the commencement of the twentieth century and a further division of land at the other side of the buildings by the making of the Rauma Railway 1920-24. The fjord terminal of the Dombås railway was created at Åndalsnes where suitable land was available without building yet another difficult bridge over the now wider Rauma river mouth. So the town gradually developed with road, rail and sea traffic. My favourite spot is a stationary railway coach, in its own little siding and platform, a dedicated Railway Chapel.

William Cecil Slingsby recorded staying there in 1875, with his sister and paid subsequent visits to this inn. Some years later *'this most delightful estate'* was bought by Mr H. O. Wills, *'whose hospitality I have since had the pleasure of enjoying'* (Slingsby). Through the subsequent century it has served as an agricultural school, periodically a guest house and now it has been refurbished in a most appropriate manner as hotel and conference/meeting place.

Although set between the main road and railway (in the early days it had a railway station) Hotel Aak is quiet and peaceful in its natural garden and offers all you could desire in food and drink. Most important of all it is served with gracious hospitality making for a glorious oasis in this mountainous world. How soon can we return, Astrid?

Trondheim in Stone

I have searched for years in anticipation of satisfying my suspense, to find where Bishop Johan Ernst Gunnerus actually died. He was enthroned as Bishop of Nidaros on 31st July 1758. He had been appointed by King Fredrik V in Copenhagen where he had been on the university staff for three years. There were 'winds of change' in Copenhagen on the death of the pious Christian VI and the accession to the throne in 1746 of his twenty three year old son, a popular, pleasure seeking man, in contrast to his strict religious father. Gunnerus had completed his university studies in Jena and Halle after Copenhagen. He remained in Jena, then as now an academic, scientific centre of learning, for a further decade writing, lecturing, preaching, developing his debating skills and broadening his interests in academic, social and scientific fields. Suddenly in 1754 Gunnerus was called to Copenhagen to be appointed 'extraordinary' professor of theology. He never actually took up that appointment. Professional jealousy crept in when he gave as many as four popular lectures a day, attracting not only university students but also many others searching for modern knowledge and thinking, presented in a way they could understand.

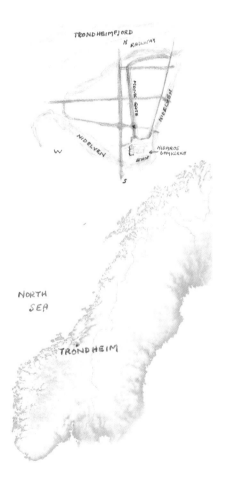

Nidaros Cathedral across Nidelva.

Husaby near Trondheim. Here Sigrid Undset lived and wrote for a time. The second book of her trilogy , 'Kristin Lavransdatter' is called 'Mistress of Husaby'.

The most impressive approach to the oldest bishopric in Norway was by sea. Some two hundred and fifty islands, the skerries, protect the one thousand six hundred kilometres of Norway's western coast line. No doubt there would be times when the uninhabited rocky outcrops would be dangerous hazards in the eighteenth century but today you may glide comfortably through on modern coastal vessels complete with modern navigational aids. I suspect that Gunnerus was not a very good sailor but his enthusiasm for his work and 'flock' spurred him forward. There would be many welcoming havens, accessible only by boat, where the young bishop would be treated like a visitor from outer space. After the usually rough stretch of Hustadvika and Stad, where I started this pilgrimage, vessels negotiate the wide, island strewn mouth of the Trondheimsfjord, moving eastwards towards the north-south mountain barrier dividing Norway and Sweden. We know that it was here, on Gunnerus' last journey that he became very ill and a few days later died but where? I think it must have been on a ship but which ship?

The fjord, deep enough for ocean going vessels, stretches 130 kilometres inland before making a great, right angled sweep northward where the fresh mountain waters of the River Nid (*Nidelva*) cross the coastal plain and meander into the sea more or less creating an island. Here thirty seven kilometres inland from the rough Norwegian Sea, King Olav Tryggvason (King Olav I, 963-1000) built a church, dedicated to St Clements, and dwellings for family, retainers and servants in the year 997. This strategic site was easily accessible by water, the most convenient method of transport a millennium ago, and food, drinking water, wool and building materials were readily available. A trading post quickly developed, naturally called Kaupanger (markets) but two decades later it was renamed Nidaros giving prominence to its situation- the river *Nid* and *os* the river mouth.

Today Trondheim is the third largest city in Norway, the modern technological capital of the country, with some 146,000 inhabitants and a student population of twenty five thousand. The intervening millennium is packed with history. For centuries it was the cultural and administrative centre of the rich area with the cathedral periodically dominant. The Cathedral retains the name Nidaros Domkirke, the most prestigious building in the city and the largest medieval building in Northern Europe.

Libraries of books have been written about the fascinating history and development of this special area of Trøndelag, bordering closely on the east with Sweden - sometimes peacefully, sometimes uneasily - and the interesting people who have passed their days there. You will find stacks of information on electronic devices if you wish. Now I want to concentrate in detail on the cathedral West Front for here is history pictured in stone, reaching back into the mists of time. The more you look the more you see. Do not hurry by to the excellent Archbishop's Palace Museum detailing the developments in the building of this famous church after ravages by fire, storm and plunder but sit peacefully and gaze at the splendour before you.

Overwhelming! Blindingly confusing! Just focus on one figure for a time and think about the people behind it- the character, the artist, the architect, the mason. Why should it be there?

Work started on the building of the church in 1070 over the site of the burial of King Olav Haraldson (King Olav II, 995-1030) killed in the battle of Stiklestad in 1030. He was declared a saint one year and five days after his death and pilgrims soon began to flock to his shrine as miraculous deeds were told. The building was completed around 1300; partially destroyed by fire and somewhat rebuilt several

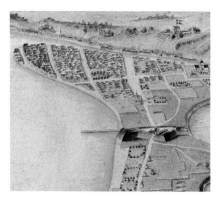

Map of Trondheim c 1730.

Trondheim c 1900.
Watercolour A. Heaton-Cooper.

King Olav Tryggvason (Olav I)

times until it was badly damaged by fire in 1531 and only an empty shell remained at the time of the Reformation of the Church. So it remained, with only a small portion usable, until the major rebuilding and restoration commenced in 1869. It was 'officially' completed in 2001 but maintenance work continues and there is much to do in a building this age and size. It will be 'completed' in 'God's good time'. I first saw the work in 1960 on my first short visit to Trondheim from a coastal steamer. The yard before the West Front was occupied by temporary drawing offices and sculptor, artist and work-men's sites. I was fascinated to see the meticulous work going on with callipers, plaster, stone and fine instruments. It is a revelation to see the frontage and new surroundings now free from scaffolding.

Take a seat beneath the trees facing the West Front, then passers-by will not disrupt your view and you may comfortably obtain refreshment from the pleasant building on your left if needed - you may get carried away by time! Appropriately we will start with the first figure on the left of the bottom row, King Olav Tryggvason, a fine figure of a man, who founded Nidaros and built St Clements Church. Born (c.968) of Norwegian stock after his father was killed, he and his mother fled the country so providing a remarkable education for a slave and then soldier. He spent some years in Sweden and in charge of a Viking vessel in 995 he landed in the Scilly Isles, south of the Cornish peninsula in the British Isles. There he was converted by a hermit seer to Christianity and he was baptised by the Archbishop of Canterbury and the Bishop of Winchester in England as he returned to Norway to reclaim his birthright and Christianize the kingdom. In chapter one we read of his gathering at Dragseidet where he forced baptism on all. It is not surprising that between his feet is the head of the slave Tormod Kark who slew his pagan master, Haakon Jarl. King Olav I died in the battle of Svolder in the year 1000.

Next to King Olav I stands Bishop Sigurd, an English Benedictine priest, born and educated in Glastonbury [a spot in *England's green and pleasant land* (William Blake's *Jerusalem*,) associated with Joseph of Arimathea and King Arthur] who was created missionary-bishop in England to accompany Olav back to Norway in 995. When the king was killed he travelled over to Sweden and eventually settled at Vaxjø becoming the church's first bishop. He converted Olof, King of Sweden in 1008.

Returning to his monastery after a missionary journey Sigfred (spelling changed in Sweden, sometimes Sigfrid, as in Oxford Dictionary, or Sigfried) found the heads of his three nephews, sent as novices from England, floating in a wooden vessel, as used on farms for storing dried cereals, in the river. He recovered the heads and claimed they could talk. When the king heard of the deed he commanded that the murderers should likewise be executed but Sigfred pleaded for their lives and even refused the blood-money produced instead. This made his mission even more successful. I wonder if he remembered the severed heads he had witnessed as he accompanied Olav Tryggvason attempting to forcibly Christianise Norway 995 - 1000? I am sure he did and the experience was turned to good.

I paid a springtime visit to Vaxjø, Småland, Sweden in 2000, tracing the early life of Carl Linnaeus (1707-1778), who attended the Cathedral School there in the early eighteenth century and eventually became the first Professor of Botany at Uppsala University. (Previously 'botany' had been included in 'medicine'). Nestling beside the modern restructured church can be seen the original Cathedral School attended by the boy from Stenbrohult Rectory some thirty miles away. (The building can be seen on the left of the church). Now I learn that the beautiful cathedral building, with its

Bishop Sigurd

Vaxsjø Cathedral, Sweden.

77

Glastonbury Abbey. An ecumenical service being held round the altar of St. Joseph of Arimathea June 2009.

Stiklestad Church with murals of the battle in 1030 AD.

distinctive copper covered spires, was erected on the site of the little wooden church built by Bishop Sigfred and the bishop appears on the city's coat of arms holding a building, the first church in Vaxjø. In the modern church is a mosaic depicting the heads of the three early martyrs, the nephews of Sigurd, Saints Unaman, Sunaman and Winaman. Bishop Sigfred died in 1045 and was buried within or near the first church.

In the centre of the row above the two figures described stands the prominent statue of St Olav (King Olav II) martyr's axe in hand. He was the son of Harald Grenske - Olav Haraldson - and his biography is so much like Olav Tryggvason's (King Olav I) it is very easy to confuse them but he was born in 995, the year Olav Tryggvason became king. After studying in England and Normandy, he was baptised in Rouen, and returned to his homeland determined to complete the conversion of Norway to Christianity begun by Olav I, with brutal tactics and psychic trickery at crucial times. He had to flee to relatives in Russia leaving a trail of memories along the way - invariably you find 'St Olav's well' pointed out today in old farms and along waysides. You know the details of the story in the foundation of the great cathedral and the enactment of his last battle in the play at Stiklestad, always commencing on St Olav's Day, 29th July. If you should be in Stiklestad at any time of year do not fail to enjoy the peace and serenity of the church, especially the mural round the apse ... I leave you to the experience.

I am captured by the second figure on the top row to the right of the lovely rose window and the central screen. King Uzziah sits in regal splendour holding in his hand a model of the defensive tower he built in Jerusalem. Now why should Uzziah be in this collection? I have long been familiar with his name, rather as a date from the Prophesy of Isaiah, *'In the year that King Uzziah died I saw the Lord, high and lifted up ...'* but here it is who is the model used for the figure of the king of Judah that delights me, that reminds me of the workmanship displayed. Just look at the pedestal!

The designer, Sivert Donali (1931-), had modelled King Uzziah on a portrait of the archaeologist and architectural historian, Gerhard Fischer (1890-1977) well known amongst the excavations and rebuilding of the cathedral. In 1965 he had published, after thirty years' work, two great volumes on the architectural history of the *Domkirke*. Fischer suffered from a great fear of heights, perhaps because he was used to archaeological digs and bending down, but his wife Dorothea (Tulla) was his closest colleague, ever at hand. Here she is permanently remembered climbing a ladder to check some detail of her husband's portrait, in communication by field telephone with her husband on the floor some distance away. Remembered! 'Behind every great man is a good woman' but that may not be true in these days of sex equality.

Similarly we have memorial touches in the figure of Bishop Sigurd whose face is modelled on the poet Aasmund Olavson Vinje and the heads of his nephews have the appearance of the architects of the reconstruction, Gudolf Blakstad, Herman Munthe Kaas and Helge Thiis, sculptured by Dyre Vaa. The thought creates a little smile when you carefully examine the otherwise gruesome picture.

I never leave Trondheim without spending some time gazing up at the south tower of the west front and giving thanks to God for the understanding he has given me through the almost unseen, graceful statue of St Gertrude of Nivelles. I have only known of her in recent years, funnily enough through my search for Gunnerus. I had never

King Uzziah

St. Gertrude of Nivelles.

Mural in Jetsmark Church, Denmark, with chapel emphasising her hospitality.

liked my name as a child. It was very rare in England during the twentieth century though my Norwegian mentor now tells me it was the third most popular name in Trøndelag in 1548. I felt looked upon with disdain as an old fashioned child, left out of games and given the tasks and responsibilities my companions did not want. I asked why I was called Gertrude and told I was named after an aunt who died when she was five years old in 1892.

It was whilst on my way to retrace Gunnerus' days in Copenhagen that I saw an interesting production of Shakespeare's 'Hamlet, Prince of Denmark'. I studied the background of the play based on a Danish legend, a story retold by Danish sailors and merchants, temporally in London delivering timber for rebuilding, to the actor/playwright. They told of their reverence for Saint Gertrude, how they prayed for her protection and gave thanks when they returned safely to harbour. A gilded figure of her gazed over the narrow sea passage between Denmark (Elsinore) and Sweden, from a niche in the wall of St Olav's Church for she was known as the patron saint of sailors and travellers.

The top figure on the right-hand tower is of St Gertrude (often spelt *Gjertrud* in Norwegian) of Nivelles, holding the abbess's staff in her right hand and an open book, suggestive of her writings and studies, in her left. Her symbol was a mouse. Here the sculptor has created rats or they would not be seen at all in this massive stone gallery, one on her garment and another on her book. I think they suggest her quiet, peacefulness and consideration for all life, small creatures but effective.

Determined to find out more about this saint, I came across many references to her, particularly in Denmark. Her name is still used in guest houses, restaurants and churches in Copenhagen and along coasts of Denmark and Norway obviously given by seafarers. I found an extensive cave shelter between Haugesund and Røldal called *'Gjertrud's Hidleren'*, a shelter for midsummer pilgrims to Røldal Church. The recently restored mural of 1474 in Jetsmark Church near Aalborg, Denmark, is remarkable. A figure complete with mice, though one hand is missing, can be viewed on the altar triptyche of Ringsaker Church on the shore of Lake Mjøsa.

I had first to find Nivelles. Leaving Geiranger one day to go over the Trollstig Way I paused at Valldal to photograph the insertion in the mountain rock of what is renowned to be the sea serpent King Olav II threw from the water as he escaped from the west coast, along Tafjord and over to Lesja, Lom and Gudbrandsdalen to Russia. Parked for a few moments at the roadside, a lady came out to offer me an apple from her tree there. We spoke for awhile and she told me she was the local doctor's wife from Belgium. I asked about Nivelles. Although she had never heard of St Gertrude or Nivelles she later provided a map of Belgium which gave me a further clue.

I flew from Birmingham to Brussels and was driven round the outskirts of the city, across the battlefields of Waterloo to the city of Nivelles in Brabant. Jeannine, my guide for the day, met me at the Collegiate Church of St Gertrude and conducted me round this remarkable building, even into parts not normally open to the public. Gertrude was born in 626 at Landen, near Nivelles to Pepin and the saintly Itta. Peppin was mayor of Austrasia, duke of Brabant and a chief political figure under the Merovingian kings.

When Pepin died in 640 the wealthy Itta was advised by Bishop Arnulf (Ørnulf) of Metz to convert her palace into an abbey. She built two adjacent monasteries in Nivelles, one for men (overseen by

Gertude's hidleren (shelter) near Røldal.

The collegiate Church of St. Gertrude, Nivelles, Brabant, Belgium 2007.

The graves of Pepin and St. Itta (Their remains have been shared out in church shrines).

The cloisters, bells and neighbouring churches in Neville.

monks from Ireland) and one for women. She appointed the twenty year old Gertrude first abbess and Itta lived with her. This placed Gertrude in a very prominent position as ruler of the city, even the head of defence - a canon in the cloisters is a reminder of this and there is still an upper room in the church, lavish with old silver, where she held court. She was a quiet, studious abbess who spent much time in devotions, reading and writing. Annually she visited all her farms round her city and this custom is continued today on the first Sunday after Michaelmas -29th September- usually the first Sunday in October. The shrine of St Gertrude is taken on an ancient carriage drawn by strong farm horses at the head of the procession. The carriage remains in the Collegiate Church of St Gertrude.

Behind the altar, down a few steps from the level of the interior of the church, completely restored by 1984, is the crypt and a narrow door. A great key opened the door. We entered and began a further stone-spiral descent, a descent into the past, almost 15 centuries ago. We passed through the crypt of the church partially burned by incendiary bombs on 14 May 1940, further down to the first abbey of 640. I stood transfixed. Here were tombs, proved by modern methods to be of the seventh and ninth centuries and it flashed on my mind that there must be some truth in many legends if we delved deep enough. To actually touch the stones and walk beside walls of the place where Gertrude had ministered to the wayfarer, to pilgrims on their way to Rome or Santiago de Compostela, kindled a flame within me and changed my attitude. She was only thirty when she resigned her office to her niece, her elder sister's daughter, and remained in the abbey until her death in 659 at the age of thirty three.

My figure of St Gertrude of Nivelles was carved in Norway of Russian oak by the wood carver, Rolf Taraldset, a few years ago, complete with two mice but on a pedestal of carved oak leaves. I have many carved oak mice in my homes for the mouse is the trade mark of Robert Thompson's Craftsmen of Kilburn, Yorkshire and I appreciate the hospitable qualities of the wood and craftsmanship, and have proved its iron-like assets of withstanding fire and water. The original copy of Gunnerus' *Flora Norvegica* I found in Oslo in 1997 is displayed in an oak bible box crafted in Kilburn, now in the Warwickshire College Library, England. It is another coincidence - carved from oak brought down in the great gale of 1987 near Kew Gardens, South Kensington, which was an acorn in 1766, the year of the publication of Part I of Gunnerus' *Flora Norvegica*.

The pedestal of Trondheim's St Gertrude is one of the most remarkable pieces on this great facade. You may not be able to see it for it is small and far away but you can take my word for it or see the official photograph in the book shop. It is unique - as far as I can see it is the only smiling figure there. The jolly pilgrim has his sack upon his back and basks in the safety of the patron saint of pilgrims.

I hope you will find your own special interest in the magnificent masterpiece of the West Front - there are so many treasures waiting for you to espy. I wonder what it feels like to 'live' with so many saints on your doorstep?

St. Gertude's tomb. (Her body is in the restored shrine in the High Altar.)

The Warwickshire 'Flora Norvegica'.

St. Gertrude's pedestral Nidaros Domkirke. The Happy Pilgrim.

83

Give me a good digestion, Lord,
And also something to digest
Give me a healthy body, Lord,
With sense to keep it at its best.

Give me a healthy mind, O Lord,
To keep the good and pure in sight
Which seeing wrong is not appalled
But finds a way to put it right.

Give me a mind that is not bored,
That does not whimper,
                whine or sigh.
Don't let me worry overmuch,
About that fussy thing called 'I'.

Give me a sense of humour, Lord,
Give me the grace to see a joke,
To get some happiness from life
And pass it on to other folk.

An Ancient Prayer from Glastonbury Abbey
Carolingian hand first used in the 8th century

This ancient prayer from Glastonbury Abbey, Somerset was first used in the 8th-century, the Carolingian Period. St. Gertude was of Carolingian descent and lived and died in the 7th-century.

I have tried to live by the message of the last verse for many years and believe that is why 'the pilgrim' of St Gertrude's pedestral caught _my_ eye.

Along the Northern Coast

My first introduction to North Norway was in 1962 when I bravely took a party of five 'old' ladies, (well, around seventy years of age) on the Express Coastal Steamer, Vesterålen, from Bergen to Kirkenes and return. We arrived in Bergen from Newcastle on 17th May, *den syttende mai*, and wondered what had happened to this colourful city in which I was becoming interested. Was it a strike or just a demonstration? There were crowds of people, some in national dress, Norwegian flags everywhere, and much excited noise as we docked in Skoltegrunnen Quay in Bergen. To make matters worse, we were called together by our tour leader who informed us he had just received a cable from his chief in London to say that he had been unable to book the meal we had been promised in Bergen that evening and he would reimburse us for the meal. So we embarked into this colourful sea of red, white and blue plus brass. I knew a quiet five star hotel, not far along Torgalmenning where my little group would get rest and refreshment until departure time for Vesterålen. Hurtigruten still leaves at 10pm.

We had a delicious meal in the old Bristol Hotel, (alas no longer in existence - It was MacDonald's the last time I looked) and learnt much about this special day on the Norwegian calendar, National Day,

Skoltegrunnen quay, Bergen.

Merchants' Houses, quayside, Bergen.

Over Bergen from Mount Ulriken.

17th May, **den syttende mai**. Norway declared itself an independent nation by the signing of the constitution of Norway at Eidsvoll on 17th May, 1814. For some years, whilst still under the domination of the Swedish king, it was a quiet celebration. The cause was taken up by such forceful, national, personalities as Henrik Wergeland (writer) and Bjørnstjerne Bjørnson (Nobel laureate 1903) focusing more round the school children and students so that their 'national independence' should not be forgotten.

From the establishment of the independent Kingdom of Norway in 1905 celebrations have been focused on the royal family, especially in Oslo. Throughout the country the school children, in national dress, with their own school bands, move like a colourful slow train through city, town or village. Now I have become part of it - the first time in Oslo when I was given a seat before the balcony of the royal palace and the Oslo school children came by, school by school, on 17th May 1973 to greet their king Olav V and little Princess Marthe Louise' first appearance. Another year I witnessed the marshalling of the schools, bands and banners from Nidaros Cathedral, an impressive, efficient train they formed past Olav Trygvasson's statue. Earlier in the morning I had taken part in the moving seamen's memorial ceremony and the placing of flags, flowers and accompanied by trumpets on the quayside and beside the seamen's museum.

The occasion I liked best was at Geiranger, a happy, smaller affair with everyone taking part from babies in perambulators (with flags, of course) to the display of new *bunad*s (national dress for women and men) and the sun shone brightly on us all as the procession twisted slowly up from the quayside to the church. (NB I used the word 'procession' here as the terrain did not permit the clearly defined sides of a 'train' (official name in Norwegian is *Barnetog*, children's train).

Today we shall join a more modern vessel of the Express Coastal Steamer (**Hurtigruten**) fleet in Trondheim, M/S Midnatsol. For more than a century a vessel has left Bergen each evening at 10pm and returned early afternoon eleven/twelve days later having sailed more than four thousand kilometres on the regular journey from Bergen to Kirkenes on the Norwegian/Finnish/Russian border. The summertime return journey Bergen-Kirkenes-Bergen is 5110 km including a detour of 146.16 km from Ålesund to Geiranger and return on the northbound journey. The vessel has up to 34 ports of call both north and south bound and conveniently for our pleasure, usually visits ports used in the night time northwards, in daytime southwards. A very special extra 4 km is added twice to the round voyage, weather permitting, from mid May to October/November,

17th May procession Geiranger.

Another festive day in Geiranger.
Author in Gudbrandsdals bunad with
cavalier and Fjord Finn 2005.

Sogneprest Runde returns for 17th May celebrations.

Trollfjord

M/S Midnatsol

a detour along the narrow, deep clefted Trollfjord. I am not sure who enjoys this most, the captain displaying his navigational skills or the passengers who hold their breath when the ship does its tight 360° pivotal turn at the head of the fjord and allows them to almost hand touch the geological features of the high mountainous walls. We were there once when the captain did two dizzying complete turns just for fun!

In 2009 I am not sure if this precise timetable is applicable for it is a bitter disappointment to find we do not have a single North Sea ferry crossing from Norway to England. Gone are the days of the 'vomiting Venus' and the 'jumping Jupiter', the leisurely commencement of an energetic climbing holiday, skiing tour or honeymoon as on Fred Olsen's M/S Blenheim or M/S Braemar. The centuries old seaway of our ancestors has been lost in the super-jet-space age.

We will creep along the interesting coast in M/S Midnatsol (16,000 tonnes, built 2003, Fosen/Rissa on Trondheimsfjord, 1,000 passengers) a very special ship built to combine and serve many purposes in a splendid manner. It is a 'working' coastal steamer carrying cargo, passengers and vehicles from port to port, as vessels have done since Richard With and Vesterålen Steamship Company in 1893 and the combination of local routes and companies in the intervening century - I hesitate to choose a word to describe its additional occupations. You may get the wrong idea if I said 'cruise ship' and expect organised games and nightclub entertainments but it has most comfortable accommodation, abundance of excellent Norwegian food and a caring staff. For me it has everything - quiet serenity, spa, library and an ever changing, living, moving panorama, most interesting shore visits and as much exercise as you require in bracing, fresh clean air.

We will commence our journey northwards from Trondheim as Bishop Gunnerus did in May 1759. The route was almost the same as the one used today, the best obviously discovered through generations of experience and seamanship in neighbouring regions. The vessel though was very, very different, considered luxurious in its time. I searched rigorously through lists of ships entering and leaving Trondheimsfjord 1759 to 1773 which might have been used by the bishop. I had erroneously presumed it was a ship owned by the Bishop himself, he was the third most important personage in Trondheim, but no single person owned just one complete ship and there was no mention of any vessel at the auction of Gunnerus' estate - he died in debt. I have visited shipyards, museums and a boatyard building replicas of eighteenth century church boats but we do know from contemporary records it was the largest cruise ship seen on the fjord, with a crew of twenty men, including eight pairs of oars. The stateroom provided ample accommodation in which Gunnerus could read and write - it is fascinating to see the change in writing style in his journal when encountering a rough stretch of sea. There would be no sailing after dark so the pastoral visits were made May to early September by the aid of the sun at midnight.

On board M/S Midnatsol.

Trondhjemfjord craft.

Leaving Trondheim along the fjord boundary between North- and South-Trøndelag we move north easterly to the fjord mouth and then creep north along the island strewn coast of South-Trøndelag. I am always loath to leave Trondheim and its most interesting fjord. To me it is still the heart of Norway. Trondheimsfjord is my favourite fjord for it has such a rich variety of seascape and landscape endowed with a wealth of history and depth of folklore through centuries. We find prehistoric reminders in rock carvings to signs of more recent history like the bitter sweet site of Falstad, school- internment camp-museum. There is rich agricultural land, cleared of stones by

Hellesvik, Frøya

Hellesvik Memorial

generations of ancestors, the stones being used for church building or walls. Now we see power stations, industrial plants, factories producing paper, chocolate, packing, freezing, drying foods and electronic equipment especially along the eastern coast of the fjord with main road and railway transport. Prestigiously Trondheim has been a religious and educational centre since the eleventh century.

Trondheimsfjord itself is 130 kilometres long, 617 m at its deepest point and contains rich marine life with at least 90 species of fish and deep water corals. It includes the shallowest cold water coral reef in the world (at 39 m) and the largest reef complex 14 kilometres long and 30 meters in height. I am intrigued by the thought of the coral sea-tree and that investigations of the coral were commenced in 1760 by Gunnerus. There are at least two note-worthy islands within the fjord, Munkholmen, a pretty little spot on a summer's day which has been both a prison and a monastery at times and Tautra with monastic remains.

We follow the way of Bishop Gunnerus on his first Pastoral Journey to visit the most northerly section of his bishopric in 1759. He found trade was booming along the North Sea coast of Trøndelag (N W Norway), particularly in timber and fish. Dried fish was exported in quantity to the Catholic areas of the Mediterranean, particularly Spain (including Portugal) and Italy where religion demanded a fish meal every Friday. The local catches had to be consumed fresh daily whereas the dried white fish from the north would be edible for years. Ships came annually, especially from Portugal, to purchase a ship load of dried cod bringing rock and stones as ballast. This material was dumped where they anchored and remains can still be seen incorporated in quaysides along the coast. They also brought men (I leave that result to your imagination).

We can still see fish being dried on the outskirts of fishing villages as it was three hundred years ago. The catch was brought ashore, cleaned, split in half and gutted and the tail ends fastened together and suspended over horizontal wires supported by crossed poles in the ground, to dry naturally on the shore. The completed structure appeared like the roof of a building, the crossed staves forming the gable ends and the grey silver scales of the fish the tiles. The dried fish - mainly *torsk* or cod - eventually looks and feels like wood before it is packed for export. This is called *stokkfisk* or *tørrfisk*. Another method of drying fish, requiring more intense labour, produces *klippfisk*. The fish is similarly cleaned, split, gutted, salted and laid to dry on the coastal rocks or cliffs (·*klippe*) and has to be individually protected from birds and weather. The traditional Christmas dish is not surprisingly a fish dish of specially prepared dried fish, *lutefisk*, which must be tasted for Viking experience.

It is a picturesque sight to see two or three fish drying frames amongst colourfully painted fishing farms on the coast. There are usually some to be seen on promontories near Bodø and always many around the islands of Lofoten, the great fishing fields of Scandinavia. Today there are freezing plants, fish processing factories and packing stations near harbours or towns and ships as moveable factories moving in tandem with a fishing fleet.

So we continue with M/S Midnatsol calling at various ports delivering goods, passengers and vehicles in exchange for goods, passengers and vehicles. An amusing game to play from the deck of the ship is to guess the contents of the cargo being driven and hoisted on board and checking the list with the purser on departure. It is even more interesting to see where the goods are going on the southbound journey – maybe exports to some far romantic place.

Trondheim Quayside in winter.

Fish drying on costal rocks. Water colour by Alfred Heaton Cooper c 1900.

Brønnøysund

Torghatten from the sea.

Torghatten from the land.

When I first visited Brønnøysund in 1962 I saw a triangular green central park in the small township where the local brass band, in smart red and white uniforms, played each afternoon as the coastal steamer brought the world to their door-step. Today we find purpose built, multi-storey office buildings stretched along the quay side, containing departmental electronic records for the whole of Norway. Brønnøysund is on a long narrow peninsular and a wide well-designed modern bridge joins neighbouring islands. The long stretch of coast line is fringed with marinas and anchorage, suitable for every size and type of sea going vessel.

Express coastal steamers often make a detour to the west of Brønnøysund so passengers may view the distinctive massive hat-shaped rock, Torghatten, and clearly see the great hole through the crown. Legends abound of Tor and the mountains but this island rock is prehistoric dating back to a much higher sea level.

I have seen the hole, 112 meters above sea level and large enough for a fully rigged sailing ship to pass through, from the land side, for an 8 kilometers long road has been constructed southwards, along the narrow peninsula from Brønnøysund. It is a steep climb to picnic in the hole but to be fully appreciated it must be seen in the distance from the sea.

The Coastal Express Steamer (*Hurtigruten*) proceeds northwards, passing Tjøtta it approaches the Island of Alsten. At the southern tip we can see the prominent church of Alstahaug, a white painted stone building from the twelfth century, extended in 1865 and recently impressively renovated to include the Petter Dass Museum.

The well loved, jocular, parson-poet was born on the neighbouring island Herøy c 1647, the son of a Dundee (Scotland) merchant,

Peter Dundas and his Norwegian wife. The merchant died when the child was around six years old and later his widow remarried and moved away leaving Petter with her sister, the wife of the priest of a nearby parish. In his teens he studied in Bergen going on to Copenhagen University there being no tertiary education in Norway. In Copenhagen he earned his fees as a tutor, as other poor Norwegians did (e.g. Gunnerus c 1737), and in due course returned as a priest to Northern Norway. In 1689 he moved to Alstahaug where he spent the rest of his life amongst the people of his extensive parish, visiting, fishing, ministering and educating.

Alstahaug from M/S Midnatsol

I cannot help smiling whenever I pass Alstahaug and think of this friendly, rotund parson, complete with ruff and gown, who had the gift of touching the hearts of his people through his poetry. He knew that a few lines of verse clung to the memory more easily than a long erudite sermon. He was familiar with the intimacies of their lives, he was one of them, and could turn his words in an attractive manner. I love the poem which includes the hostess' preparation for the visitation of important guests, perhaps Dass himself. She takes out the hides, furs, and woollen rugs from the guest house (the farms consisted of many single storey wooden buildings for special purposes) and shakes them in the fresh air. The poet describes, in his own inimitable rhythm, how the army of invading mutineers (lice, mice and such like lodgers) are cast away like fleeting horsemen. (*Rytteri* –horsemen, rhyming with *Mytteri* – mutineers).

Alsten from the south.

Petter Dass' most famous work, I think, is '**Nordlands Trompet**' (The Trumpet of Nordland). It clearly trumpets praise and clear insight of the geography, nature, fish and animals and people's joys and sorrows of this remarkable land.

Approaching The Seven Sisters Mountains, Alsten.

Sandnessjøen Bridge

Sandnessjøen Bridge in the distance.

We see more of the mountainous background of Alstahaug as we continue north, parallel to the coast of Alsten and its impressive mountain chain consisting of 'The Seven Sisters'. You may see the seven mountain tops veiled in lace-like snow or you may see them holding white hands with each other but you will always find a glacier between them (six glaciers). The smallest mountain is Stortinden (910 metres) – I think that is a joke for the smallest to be called 'the great peak'- the most southerly and just behind Alstahaug. The highest (1,072 metres), is the most northerly, regally situated at the head of Botnfjord and not surprisingly named Botnkrona, 'the crown of Botn'.

We may curtsey to the ancient 'maidens' on our four hour journey from Brønnøysund to Sandnessjøen as we make our way to this port on the north west tip of Alsten, at the mouth of the Botnfjord. Today a most noteworthy bridge, Helgeland Bridge, spans this wide gap joining Sandnessjøen to the mainland and opening up a useful and now important, hinterland with the towns of Mosjøen and Mo I Rana.

Sandnessjøen has grown beyond recognition in the last fifty years. It was in the very bright light of a midsummer noon in June 1962 I first saw this delightful village and perhaps thought of retirement. The 'main road' was the sea scattered with rocks and some inhabited islands and a church at the opposite end of the village street to the harbour which was a quite hectic terminal for many busy little ships.

I returned in July 1970 by road and stayed at 'The Seven Sisters' Hotel' so beautifully decorated with local paintings. This situation gave me the opportunity to visit the island of Dønna a short ferry ride away. It was one of the most radiant days I have ever spent in Norway. The placid brown cows were leisurely ruminating in the buttercup strewn bright green pastures beneath a cloudless azure sky.

The Seven Sisters Mountains

Alstahaug Church

Geirangerfjord – newly named oil-rig rescue vessel anchored overnight.

Behind me was the white painted twelfth century stone church with its black 'onion' spire, protected by a few low silver birch trees with shimmering pendant leaves caught in a gentle breeze and before me the distant snow covered mountains. Here was 'peace' encaptured for a brief time.

My next opportunity to visit Sandnessjøen by land was in 2003. I had passed by sea several times in the nineteen nineties to Svalbard and Finnmark but had previously been stranded two decades in Singapore.

Alas! There was no 'Seven Sisters' Hotel'! There was a hotel but the stars had gone out. The main street was very much busier; many houses had been built with streets stretching inland, business buildings and offices thronged the quayside and there was even a traffic island and traffic lights. I looked from my bedroom window and directly opposite was an oil rig rescue vessel which I had seen named beneath the 'Seven Sisters' Waterfall' in Geirangerfjord a

Dønna Church

Calypso bulbosa (Latin)
NORNE (Norwegian)

few months before. I never expected to see it again. Here was a clue to the changing appearance of not only Sandnessjøen but several communities along the north-west and northern coasts of Norway.

The North Sea had long been a rich sea bed for fish giving a plentiful supply of food for home and export and by products for fashion and pharmaceuticals. Then suddenly the North Sea produced a terrific bonus gift, lifting Norway amongst the greatest in the world. – the third largest producer of oil and natural gas in the world. Oil was first found south of Bergen in 1968 and production commenced in 1970. With improved technology and exploration fields have been opened up even into the Arctic. Coastal towns developed as supply bases, transport, communications and health centres. The rigs cannot be seen from the coast.

The name of the oilfield directly west of Sandnessjøen particularly delights me, Norne. Most fields have names of legendary figures like Troll, Kristin, and Åsgard but Norne (*Calypso bulbosa*) is a rare, slender, 10 cm high orchid which I found in Sweden on the same latitude as Sandnessjøen in Norway, in June 1999 when coming to Norway by the route Carl von Linné took in 1732, recorded in his 'Lapland Journey' from Uppsala to Saltfjorden and Sørfolda.

I spotted this delicacy first amongst the light undergrowth in a damp forest near the coast. The three narrow pointed sepals and two of the petals are a beautiful pinky/mauve colour whilst the enlarged lip, the insect landing platform, is wider and white, the single bloom elegantly hanging over on the fragile stem.

Along the Arctic Coast

We now reach the narrowest part of Norway, the long strip between mountains and island protected coast, merely 30 to 40 kilometres to the Swedish frontier in a few places, as we approach the Arctic Circle, (66° lat.). The coast is 1,609 kilometres so edging the longest mountain chain in Europe. It is incredibly indented with fjords so it is impossible to give an exact measurement. Well, almost impossible, some student may have time and patience to do so with the aid of modern technology. Similarly the islands and skerries cannot be counted. It has long been ascertained that 70% of the land consists of mountains, approximately 2% urban development areas, 3% arable land the remainder being water. One third of the mountains are to be found in the Arctic.

Just over the Arctic Circle lies Ørnes, an interesting town, which I remember from 1962 as a very small colourful village. In the early morning light of a May day, the sea was placidly silver and there were very few people although signs of a few fishing boats. Three or four people were there – they stopped to chat and watch if there were any passengers leaving the ship, it was M/S Vesterålen that time. There was no way to Ørnes except by sea.

M/S Midnatsol 2004

Returning in 1998, by 'the back door', the once dream town was unrecognisable, only the sky-line of the mountain background remains unchanged. A coastal road and tunnel had been constructed and the hydro-electric plants in the Glomfjord area were prominent and I by-passed Ørnes without realising it. The new coastal road continued to Bodø but I turned eastward along the shore of Saltfjorden and the famous Saltstraumen, the turbulent tidal current which streams through the 150m strait four times a day, to Rognan at the head of Saltdalsfjorden. The next day I tried to reach Ørnes from the land side but the Saltfjell National Park was impassable – my journey ended on a distant edge of Svartisen Glacier with magnificent views over Saltdal.

I have passed Ørnes many times since on M/S Midnatsol and found it an enlarged prosperous town with many signs of the oil/gas field and accompanying services.

We continue our imaginary journey on M/S Midnatsol searching for the spirit of Bishop Gunnerus though we have set aside the exploration of the exact place where he died.

A few weeks ago there came into my possession a delightful, delicate watercolour, the water streamed across the foreground in smooth shades of warm blue, grey and white. The middle line was of distant hills, islands, rocks and skerries, in blue grey stretching into paler almost non existent blue. To the untrained eye the upper half of the picture appears blank but look carefully and it is a joy to behold, especially when you recognise the image. There is a very, very pale mauve / blue haze upon the mountains. Look again and there, piercing the mist and shining above are the indomitable peaks of the snow covered Lofoten Wall.

Lofoten wall. Water colour by Alfred Heaton Cooper

There is no doubt it is the artist's view from the Saltfjord, near Bodø, looking towards the mountains on the Lofoten Islands which appear congregated in a massive impenetrable wall. Alfred Heaton Cooper (1864-1929) painted the picture around nineteen hundred. I have the sketch he made at the time, fortunately rescued recently from attic clutter by his grandson John Heaton Cooper. Alfred was a Lancashire man who married a Norwegian lady from Balestrand, Sognefjord, where they lived for a time before returning to the English Lake District. The modern Heaton Cooper Studio, Grasmere, displays the work of four generations of Heaton Coopers but it is Alfred's Norwegian scenes which hold my heart and keep Norway for me in foreign places.

Bishop Gunnerus anchored within the Arctic Circle in Saltfjorden for the first time in May 1759 and records in his 'Visitation Register' the confirmation of Rasmus Jacobsen of Saltdal on 16th May. The Parish of Salten was an extensive diocese bordering on Sweden, at its narrowest point only 4.8km from the head of Tysfjorden at Hellemoborn to the Swedish frontier.

The parishioners would have gathered at the head of the Saltfjord to welcome the bishop on his first visit. It is a reminder of the bishop's stalwart character to read his actual record at this place, as at several other spots later. The writing is frequently untidy, difficult to read and blotchy in places – evidence of an unstable surface, as on a pitching ship. Easily discernible are the times when a new quill is substituted – a clear reminder of the vast changes in calligraphy and stationery materials over the years.

This very busy area round the mouth of the Saltfjord is no longer part of the ancient See of Nidaros but the seat of the bishop of northern

Fish drying on racks near Bodø 2007.

Fish drying in the Lofoten Isles.

Norway/ Bodø. This modern city was a small fishing village of 200 souls when it was established in 1816 and remained so until around 1860 when it was blessed by the warm Gulf Stream bearing great herring catches. Subsidiary industries developed, the coastal express service made regular visits with freight and passengers, the population expanded until it is now the capital of Nordland County. The main road over Saltfjellet was still closed by snow in the winter months until into the 1980s but today there is road and rail connections inland to Trondheim and Oslo.

On my first visit in 1962 Bodø was a struggling city and the only prominent sight to be shown visitors from the Express Coastal Steamer was the newly completed cathedral (1956) and to hear an organ recital. The city was rising, like the phoenix from the ashes, after disastrous treatment during WW2. The large natural harbour protected by islands from the open sea, at times vicious, has been rebuilt and the airfield enlarged and thoroughly established. It is a modern haven involved in oil/natural gas industries, a great commercial hub - not only for sailors and fisher folk but birds and fish. The marinas attract vessels of every description for the ships are still the most convenient form of transport for work and pleasure and hundreds are anchored by the many piers.

Flocks of birds gather for food and rest on their way south to warmer climes and I remember spending hours one late August day, quite recently, sitting on M/S Midnatsol watching the birds prepare to migrate. First there were trial flights and flight tests for leadership, then jostling for place. Tests were repeated each time another group or family joined. Test runs departed and returned. The black chattering birds covered some fishing vessels, regrouped and were organised, there were disagreements – I could not hear the noise but I could see

Lofoten Fishing Boat.

it by the fluttering of wings. The flight of starlings was an amusing sight but the departure of the black cloud was a welcome sight to fisher folk.

From Bodø to the apparently sharp speared armoured barrier across our northern route we must cross a particularly rough stretch of sea, the wide mouth of the Vestfjord. On my favourite map around the extreme westerly tip is marked as 'the strongest sea current in the world', Moskstraumen. I have visited the most southerly village of Å but I notice 'Hell' is marked closer to the surging sea and would point out that the Norwegian word means 'fortunate' or 'good luck'. The skilful coastal navigators take us swiftly over the broad fjord and we find the Lofoten Wall is not an impenetrable barrier but a conglomeration of islands, the Lofoten and Vesterålen Islands.

Lofoten Wall in the far distance.

M/S Midnatsol creeps along the south coast of the first group of islands, stopping where necessary at the more populous areas like Stamsund and Svolvær before passing between islands to the narrow Raftsundet. The famous Trollfjord previously mentioned, is west, round behind an island, at the entrance to the Raftsund. Our working vessel continues round and between islands in Vesterålen making a stop at Harstad, a town which has gained in importance in the last half century and is the popular home of many of our sea-faring friends and acquaintances. Nearby is the particularly old Trondenes Church, the most northern medieval stone church in Norway, occupying the site of two previous wooden churches.

The Lofoten Islands is not a place to visit! It is a place to stay and explore. As a world traveller I can tell you, it is high on my dream list. The islands have everything – history, literature, colour, charm, peace, mountaineering, water sports in abundance and the people have a

A typical fishing village.

Vågen Church

joyful, musical exuberance touched with a tinge of old world sadness. A few hours' visit is not enough to give you a true feeling of this 'other world'. The fishing village of Henningsvær has an enchanting setting on islands joined to the mainland by bridges. The red and white painted houses, studios, warehouses are shoulder to shoulder and most have a boat near the door. The hotel is there, like an old village inn in England, the centre of community affairs, and it has everything you could wish for, food – especially fish-'par excellence'.

To explore the islands in October was the most colourful holiday I have ever had. There were no noisy crowds, roads were quiet and nature wore her rich autumnal colours, especially the rowans, brackens and heathers. We are reminded on seeing the large Vågen wooden church, between Kabelvåg and Svolvær, how last century it was completely filled by men in March before the fishing fleet left harbour for their seasonal 'harvest' of the northern waters-the women and children were left outside. Today a new 'industry' has developed here, as in many parts of Norway on previously farmed land; the fishermen have refurbished their coastal cottages and rented them to tourists.

North Norway had begun to be part of 'the global village some forty years ago, not only with the discovery of vast quantities of oil but also with the foresight of statesmen. We have seen how Norway has developed, in general, from the sea inland, the sea providing the only method of communication for some communities for centuries. The younger generation no longer wanted to farm their ancestors' lands or fish in their fathers' boats. What would happen to the most northerly counties of Troms and Finnmark if all the people gradually drifted away? The hinterland is very barren and unproductive – a large proportion covered by arctic tundra, mainly lakes, tarns and rivers.

The Sami (Lapp) family used to eke a living by reindeer herding and breeding. Thirty years ago they had to drive them in summer to fertile island pastures and I believe they still do today with the aid of military transport. Not as many herders are needed for they enjoy their scooters and snowmobiles so saving manpower. I visited schools in Kautokeino and Karasjok in May 1973 and felt the excitement as whole families were packing for their summer migration with their reindeer. I do not think many of those teenagers will have remained in their home areas today. TV and films were opening up their world and they wanted to see for themselves.

An experienced minister of defence, the *Storting* (the Parliament) representative of his native Lofoten Islands, Haakon Kyllingmark (1915-2003) recognised this problem soon after WWII. He knew that a sparsely populated Finnmark should be peacefully defended and he construed that this could be done by air transport within Norway. Airports were an expensive impossibility but with the light aircraft now available, small landing/take-off strips could be used.

Kyllingmark as a minister in The Ministry of Transport and Communications inaugurated such popular services, hopping from one small centre to another. The first four strips were opened in 1968 – Mo i Rana, Sandnessjøen, Brønnysund and Namsos-each being 840m by 30m, where as a commercial strip at that time required 2,600m by 60m. Lofoten and Vesterålen opened in 1972. There are about 25 strips today. The grateful populace amusingly dubbed the flights 'Chicken Runs' (*kylling* – chicken; *mark* – field, run). We spent Christmas Day 2006 on M/S Midnatsol anchored in Altafjord watching these happy little 'dragonflies' land, turn and take-off again.

Tromsø

Hammerfest

Honningsvåg

The northway continues and pauses again at the exciting city of Tromsø occupying a large island in the middle of Balsfjord. Here is another remarkable bridge joining the city to the mainland and providing an aerial entrance to the Cathedral of the Arctic. The lovely white triangular building, two sides of which form the steeply pointed roof and almost reach the ground at sea level. The shape of the church is like the tip of an iceberg, and exactly matches the mountain top behind when viewed from the city market place.

A recent addition to the landscape, particularly on islands and near populated out posts on the coast is the wind-park. The wind vanes are seen rotating constantly in the breezy regions supplying clean power even to areas which could not be reached from earlier sources. Will 'climate change' affect the future wind supply?

Hammerfest has changed considerably over the last half century. It was a small one street fishing town with one of the first frozen fish factories in the world. Now the entrance to the larger town is congested with extensive natural gas and liquifying plants and workers' residential accommodation and social facilities.

The opportunity to visit North Cape will be provided at Honningsvåg on the island of Magerøy, a most fascinating island which I long to explore. It was at Honningsvåg I first tasted whale meat. I had visited the tiny fishing village, crouched around the bay sheltered from the north by gentle fertile hills rising to the flat, rocky mountain plateau of the North Cape, several times before but this was special. I had come as far as Kåfjord by road and ferry but here the car had to be left and a passenger ferry taken to Honningsvåg. There I stayed in the hotel over a daylight night. I heard of work in progress on the construction of an undersea tunnel which would eventually join the Magerøy Island to the mainland and eliminate the passenger ferry. Returning in 2004, three times, I found the town of Honningsvåg unrecognisable and could not find the hotel where I had stayed and experienced the beef-like fish. Today it is an important, large fishing port with its excellent harbour and the Norwegian State College of Fisheries and a unique tourist attraction reached by air, land and sea.

The undersea tunnel was opened in 1999 making an impressive difference to Magerøy.

The reindeer herds from Karasjok still spend the summer months on the island, helped there by military truck but what a terrific sight to see them swim back, with their calves, to the mainland and winter quarters. No! You will not meet them in the tunnel but must be very careful driving in the mountain pastures. You may, like the reindeer, be pestered by mosquitoes midsummer. The insects lay their eggs in

Magerøy

En route, Honningsvåg to North Cape April 2004.

Mehamn Quay

reindeer fur and you frequently see the animals rubbing themselves against rocks in a natural attempt to stop the irritation. Be prepared! It is worth it.

Bishop Gunnerus recorded in his journal his visit to Magerøy on 7th July 1759. The remains of the medieval church are at Kjelvik, a short distance from present day Honningsvåg Church which was built in 1844. The church was the only building which remained standing after the town was razed by fire towards the end of WWII. We leave peacefully by our Hurtigruten dream ship and cross the wide mouths of the great Porsanger and Laksfjords, passing the strange rock, church-like formation, rising from the sea, to Mehamn.

Here we are in one of the most northerly fishing villages of mainland Europe. Mehamn is typical of a handful of coastal villages which have been resurrected along the edge of the Barents Sea since the firey devastations of 1945. They face the Russian sea-way to the Atlantic Ocean and the western world. A glance at the map shows how wise and far seeing Kylling was for the communities' comfort and convenience by the provision of air transport.

Berlevåg, across Tanafjord, has been protected by a special mole, with a narrow opening, from the ferocious ravages of the Barents Sea. I found when crossing from Svalbard some years ago, the local fisherfolk called this sea 'the Devil's Dance floor' and I am not surprised. The 'history' of the Berlevåg Male Voice Choir is an encouraging example of social, Social Service.

Similarly Båtsfjord, and Vardø and Vadsø on Varangerfjord have been restored during the last half century. Kirkenes, the nearest Norwegian town to Russia, Finland and Sweden is rather special.

I remember standing on the quayside in May 1962 and seeing iron ingots for the first time in my life. Ten years later I saw iron ore in Kiruna, Sweden, and travelled on the ore train over to Norway for the ore had to be exported through Narvik as the Gulf of Bothnia froze in winter. Sydvaranger attempted to develop similarly but it is no longer active. The last time I was there was Christmas 2005 the remaining slag heaps were disguised by a thin covering of snow. It was a memorable experience to join in Kirkenes Church Harvest Festival one Sunday morning whilst visiting on M/S Midnatsol October 2005. 'Harvest' is a church festival I have missed for many years. It was a happy, joyous, colourful service with the English church decorated with local produce and the hymns of thanksgiving rang loud and clear, '*All is safely gathered in ere the winter storms begin...*'

Naturally carved rock Cathedral.

There had been no harvest thanksgiving for me in the tropics for thirty years of perpetual summer and now we joined in the far north-eastern corner of the arctic. The produce brought by the children was indicative of the area of Lapland - fish, fruit from the forest, a few local vegetables, a bundle of wood ... and knitted woollen mittens. Two small boys brought hand carved pictures and it was moving to see them run to the altar at the end of the service to repossess the craft and time they had given thanks for. '*For all thy gifts we thank thee Lord ...*'

Mehamn 71° N Lat.

From the Arctic
down the Eastern Valleys

We will leave the Barents Sea and the borders of Norway, Russia and Finland behind us and take the overland route southwards. We shall not find the populous towns or the industries we found on the coast but nature offers us treasures of another kind.

Bishop Gunnerus in the mid eighteenth century travelled as far as this to the north-east, mainly by sea but here he travelled some distances by coach to visit remote Lapp communities and make contact with missionary teachers who had studied in Trondheim.

On the overland journey Gunnerus had been able to observe the wild life and to collect some plants for a garden and some specimen for his developing herbarium in Trondheim. I am excited today as I write (June 2009) in anticipation of a coming publication of digitalized photographic details of Gunnerus' own herbarium. Some names were new to the country and identified only after being forwarded to Professor Oeder in Copenhagen - *Veratrum album v. lobelianum* and *Primula sibirica*.

At the time King Fredrik V appointed Gunnerus to Trondheim (1758) Norway was under Danish rule. It was the period following

Cypripedium calceolus. Lady's slipper orchid on Flora Danica plate and tureen.

Flora Danica wine glass bath.

Carl Linneaus (1707–1778). Portrait in oils by L. Pasch after A. Rooslin, 1775, copied for Sir Joseph Banks, now in the Linnean Sosiety of London. (Linnea borealis on table corner.)

the Reformation and dedicated men were especially needed on the periphery of the kingdom to spread knowledge on the one hand and receive informative details of minerals, plants, indeed anything of value, on the other. This was the purpose of sending Professor Oeder to Norway in 1755. Oeder, the compiler of the first ten volumes of *Flora Danica*, the illustrations used to this day on the delightfully, accurate decorations on Royal Copenhagen porcelain, spent a friendly period in Trondheim.

From 1761 onwards Gunnerus and Carl von Linné had corresponded. Gunnerus had sent specimen and questions to the great botanist in Uppsala. Although the two men never met, a warm friendship developed between them, correspondence being carried by colleagues and students travelling the long road, in those days, Trondheim – Uppsala – Trondheim. On becoming a Fellow of the Linnean Society of London in 1999 my first request was to see these letters and the late Professor W. T. Stearn, author of 'Botanical Latin', took me into the Society's vault in London to view them. Linnaeus on one occasion wrote to Gunnerus,

> *"You alone reveal both of God's books - His written word and His word of nature. At the same time your enlightenment is like a great northern light more than any other bishop in Europe. May the great triune God long keep you sound and healthy."*

It is not surprising therefore that Linnaeus should name one of the new found plants, brought or sent to him by his students who travelled most of the known world as chaplain or doctor aboard vessels of the Swedish East India Company, in honour of Gunnerus. It was after reading the fascinating book *Felix Arabia* (Hansen,T 1964) recounting the Danish expedition of 1761-67 and the controversy which occurred between Carsten Niebuhr, the only member of the expedition who returned, and Linnaeus that I became interested in the names of plants. Peter Forsskål, a favourite student of Linnaeus, had sent him some specimen and the professor named one raised from seed, in memory of him, Forsskalea. Niebuhr was horrified that a stinging nettle should be named in honour of the natural leader of the group. On careful consideration of the specimen, Linnaeus had indeed made a suitable choice, for Forsskål himself had described it as stubborn, wild, obstinate and angular – the characteristics which had carried that expedition forward.

This incident made me curious about the plant Linnaeus named after Bishop Johan Ernst Gunnerus. This quest has sent me on a world wide research. I easily found it referred to in an encyclopaedia as 'the largest leaved flowering plant in the world native of the southern hemisphere'. The first specimen I found was in the Royal Horticultural Society Garden at Wisley, apparently a large over grown rhubarb plant without any flowers. I anticipated, the flowers would be on upright stems with panicles of flowers well above the leaves to attract fertilising assistants. This would mean they had to be 3 to 4m tall.

The leaves made a complete semi-circular arbour of leaves and it was only when I crept inside to investigate the stem of leaves and likely flowers that I actually saw the flower. It emerged directly from a rooted clump in the ground, rhizome-like, developing into a large, compact ovoid shape like a gigantic fir-cone. I discovered it actually consisted of hundreds of tightly packed flowers. I counted 360 florets on one cone growing beside a stream in a Warwickshire garden. They were an unattractive murky, pinky brown colour. Then suddenly for two to three days the conical head was covered with vivid red, fine hair-like stamen. The dull flower became exciting and would eventually

Celebrating the 300th anniversary of the birth of Carl von Linné in the Botanic Garden, Singapore.

With professor from Uppsala, Swedish Embassy representative and Director Singapore Botanic Garden August 2007.

Examening Linnean memorabilia in Singapore 2007.

Gunnera chilensis in a Warwickshire garden about ten years ago.

A hint of red stamen appearing on the above plant.

The general appearance is rhubarb-like but there is no similarity in the flower. Here it is completely red but will only remain so a few days.

produce thousands of seeds and minute orange berries, rarely seen because of the dense shade and protection provided by the leaves on their thick, woody stems.

Gunnera chilensis (=*tinctoria*) has been introduced into the northern hemisphere in the last decade or two as an ornamental shrub though its flowers are rarely noticed. The large heavy leaves die back completely protecting the fruit, decay provides compost and prevents the seeds from spreading. I have seen specimen in botanical gardens world wide and recently I have seen it growing in its natural state in Chile, thanks to the modern Norwegian M/V Fram, based on the plan of Nansen's arctic exploration vessel. The plant was disappointing though growing in abundance along roadsides and on the lower slopes of the Andes, always close to water, it was not as large as I had expected. The flower cones stood up like weathered stalagmites for leaves had been pruned and only a few left decaying. We learned from the local Chilean botanist that the stem of the leaves is used for food, either raw or cooked and the inside did look like bamboo. He laughed at the hairy stems being called spikes but I was not prepared to try. There is now scientific proof that this was ancient food even known to dinosaurs.

Recently I have found that Bog Gardens were popularly designed in the grounds of large Cotswold estates in the nineteenth and twentieth centuries. In some cases they have been neglected for years and thrived enormously. Now in National Trust Gardens they are guarded. I could stand comfortably within the enclosure of one plant at Coughton Court, Worcestershire and examine at close quarters the massive flowers. In early spring, what will be the flower appears like a coconut, brown and fibrous, at the ground-level base of the plant. This gradually unfolds and develops into the complicated cone-shaped cylinder of florets. As the central stem grows so too the florets shoot out 1 to 2 cm and this shoot is covered with a myriad of seeds which ripen to orange. There can be 80,000 florets packed in one flower producing 250,000 seeds. The whole flowering system is majestically, protectively surrounded by stout stems bearing thick, dark green fluted leaves up to two or three metres broad and two metres high. I have seen fruiting stems 50 cms long but they are no longer upright but recumbent.

The cultivated plants in England were far superior to the wild ones growing along the ditches in Chile. Beware! In New Zealand, where they were introduced, they are now overgrown, a menace and are being cleared, with difficulty. The gigantic plants are so large and shady that nothing else will grow near them.

Open stem revealing flesh of Gunnera chilensis which can be eaten raw or cooked. Notice outer layer is very dry.
Chile November 2008.

Gunnera chilensis flowers at various stages of development Central Chile November 2008.

Gunnera margellanica growing profusely in NTNU Botanic Garden at Svinvik, Todalsfjord within the diocese of Trondheim.

The flower is so small it can only be seen with difficulty between the curator's thumb and finger.

Gunnera tinetoria struggling to survive in the 'cold house' in Singapre Boyanic Garden. (5 years old)

Further south from Chile, on the island of Tierra del Fuego, beside the Straits of Magellan we found another *gunnera*, quite different. This was a mass of delicate foliage with a minute flower, almost invisible to the naked eye, growing beneath. The plants creep along the ground like strawberry stolon and the leaves are similar in shape to the strawberry leaf but both the flower and leaf are like tiny, miniature leaves of gigantic, *G. chilensis* ; the flower colour is similar too but the leaf has a tinge of purple underneath. **Gunnera margellanica** is named after the Straits of Magellan but the natives dub it 'devils' strawberry' which gives an idea of size, shape and taste.

This lovely ground cover does grow in Norway because it thrives in an ideal position, very similar to its original habitat, but on a cliff beside a fjord, not the Magellan Straits. The narrow sea passage was discovered in 1520 by the Portuguese navigator Ferdinand Magellan in the service of Spain. I had found it an exciting sight to first see G. margellanica carpeting the brow of the steep hillside above the Todalsfjord, in Svinvik Botanic Garden, within the diocese of Trondheim.

Between these two specimens of *gunnera* we should be able to gather almost any characteristics of Johan Ernst Gunnerus, as seen by Carl Linnaeus from the small to the great. He had developed from a mini-herbalist, helping his doctor father collecting for his 18th century pharmacy, a fluent child classicist in Christiania (now Oslo), through studies, teaching and writing in philosophy, natural science, mathematics, Greek and Hebrew in Copenhagen and Jena, to theology. This subject bound the Bishop of the North's talents and deepening interests in the world and people around him, together into the mature Gunnerus.

We can now move southwards overland on European Route 6 (E6) along the border between the Norwegian county of Finnmark and Finland and over the barren Finnmarksvidda to Lakselv at the head of the great north-south Porsangerfjord. It was here I had the most delicious fresh salmon and cucumber sauce I have ever tasted – not surprising, as Lakselv means Salmon River and the water cascades down the valley from the *vidda* like a torrent of molten silver.

The E6 follows the coast through Alta, bypasses Tromsø and the Lofoten Islands to Narvik. Of course we could take 'Chicken Runs' and cover the distance by air – a very interesting, quick journey if you have a map on your knees and see the thousands of lakes and acres of ice and snowfields beneath you.

A short distance after Fauske the road enters Saltdalen, at the head of Saltfjorden. At Fauske, a congested, busy junction today, a detour can be made to Bodø on the coast, with its shipping and airport facilities, by taking the right-hand, westerly road beside the fjord. Alternatively you may choose the left-hand turn from E6 which leads

Gunnera chilensis, Chile 2008.

Coughton court, Gunnera chilensis towers above the 2 metre + viking with petit English ladies.

Cypripendium calceolus.
Lady's slipper orchid (English)
Marisko (Norwegian)

Early frost (October) in Saltdalen with red
rods in place to meter depth of snow.

to Sulitjelma, the mountain top mining village bordering Sweden. Do enjoy the clear views of Saltdalsfjorden towards the Saltstraumen and Bodø before reaching the town of Rognan where a comfortable, convenient stop may be made.

Forty kilometres up the road from Rognan you will find Saltdal Touristsenter. At the modern complex the road to the left goes to Graddis, Sweden, beside the note-worthy Junkerdalen, a botanist's paradise.

I first found my way into Junkerdalen on 16th June 1999 and have been many times since. It is no place for jogging or even a quick walk. Every step reveals new gems and I have seen differences in growth and development between visits although they have usually been around the same time of year. Most outstanding were the groups of orchids, *Cypripedium calceolus*, standing quite near the stony path, on strong, upright stems, holding out the flower head as though offering a slipper to a lady. I had seen many specimen of orchids in my years in equatorial Singapore; I had tended fragile, delicate *cypripedium* (Lady's slipper) in the tropics but nothing as bold and commanding as these in Junkerdalen. Perhaps these were Viking Ladies' slippers, not Parisienne Ballerinas'!

Cypripedium calceolus L (Marisko = Mary's shoe) grows to a height of 40cm on a sturdy, downy covered green stem around which the ovoid pointed, deeply veined, bright green leaves are sheathed. The stalk usually bears one flower, occasionally two, with a strong, robust, bright golden yellow lip spotted with red inside and dark red-brown petals and sepals protectingly bowing over it. '*Calceolus*' refers to the limestone enriched soil it likes and here the river dashes and gurgles over smoothed limestones, as I have described in Wharfedale,

England. L indicates Carl von Linné was the first person to describe this specimen. Gunnerus also includes it in Flora Novegica (1766) and James Sowerby in English Botany (1790) reported,

> *'It is confined to some remote and little frequented woods in the North of England'*

... the woods I knew as a young child.

It is interesting to note that 'Lady's slipper' had been over gathered and died out in England but a decade ago it had been secretly replanted and protected in the area where Sowerby knew it. Please respect the plants' privacy and permit a natural life-span for generations.

From our walk in 'Paradise Garden' (Junkerdalen) we return to route E6 and soon cross the Arctic Circle on Saltfjellet with its modern Arctic Tourist Centre. We skirt the east side of the Saltfjell-Svartisen National Park and pass through Mo I Rana and Mosjoen, previously mentioned on our journey northwards, and down Namsdalen, where the road and railway accompany the River Namsen to Grong, the salmon fisherman's Mecca. We continue on E6, straight ahead towards Trondheim, whilst the river turns westward to the coast at Namsos, but there are many interesting diversions before we reach the city again.

With plenty of time to wander and to pause I like to turn left on reaching Lake Snåsa (*Snåsavatnet*) and drive to the little town and lovely church of Snåsa (especially note the adjacent wonderful old parsonage/farm). Bishop Gunnerus frequently visited this area where the local priest was a personal friend and together they collected plants and specimen. Gunnerus had made a special point

This illustration of Cypripendium calceolus is by James Sowerby and appears first in the first issue of 'English Botany' (1790). It is not as complete as Oeder's example as on Flora Danica porcelain shown on page 110 which includes the root system.

Svartisen Glacier from inland in Saltdalen region.

Snåsa Pasonage/Farm

Lilies-of-the-valley, Snåsa.
Convallaria majalis
Liljekonvall (Norwegian)

in requesting his clergy to collect as much local information, names, uses and habitats of plants, birds, fish … from their parishioners. It is this localised information which makes *Flora Norvegica* so interesting today, the same plant having diverse names and uses in different parts of the country. You may wisely choose to continue down this side of Lake Snåsa and rejoin E6 at Steinkjer. From here on you are in the area of the great Trondheimsfjord.

Southwards from Steinkjer on the E6 an inner arm of the Trondheimsfjord may be glimpsed beyond the railroad and modern industrial buildings but in 8km you may branch right on 761 or right on 755 in a further 8km and detour along the main north coast of the actual fjord. I love to pause at Jægtvolden and gaze across the kindly fjord and see the remarkable agricultural land. This good soil filled the Norwegian 'bread basket' for several centuries. Nearby, at Sakshaug are two churches – one small twelfth century church, obviously built using the local stones from the clearing of the fields, and a larger one across the road signifying the later state need for a church large enough to hold the registered population. The name, Jægtvolden, suggests the prosperity of the farmers – *"Jægt"* a larger ship; *"volden"* a bank, natural quayside - the traditional vessel for journeying to church or even to Trondheim and Bergen. We had a pleasant afternoon rest by a picnic table at a little quay here with several boat houses. We could see the two churches higher on our left, the placid fjord before us and the well-tilled ground between.

Returning to the main road, along the fjord shore, you will approach the town of Verdal and see well signposted roads, eastwards (left, if coming from the north) to Stiklestad, the site of the battle which the losers won/the victors lost on 29th July 1030. *"St Olav lost his last battle and won a halo".*

Many pilgrims visit the ancient Battlefield which now has an adjacent modern purpose-built cultural centre including museum, shop, cafeteria and very comfortable hotel and open-air theatre with a natural open stage – all a spin off from the present day prosperity. I remember it as a rough, uneven field with just a small post office in a corner where I could dispatch a letter to myself in England with a stamp I had bought elsewhere showing the battle in blue. (I may add, the letter posted in 1973 is still unopened in my collection in Singapore 2009).

To me the focal point is the twelfth century church. Last year we were privileged guests to see the annual presentation of the musical play *'Olav den Hellige'* (Saint Olav) on the eve of Olsok (St Olav's day). Before the play we attended the church service and our dear friend and guide took us around the church. I did remember the striking, vivid interior decorations of the death of King Olav II,

Prosperous farms beside Trondheimsfjord. Sakshaug churches on left.

Murals in Stiklestad Church.

A Selbumillstone at Selbusjøen. Feb. 2002.

round the apse behind the altar. Now the battlefield pictures were faded and subdued. I was told this was due to the chalk backgrounds of the murals and I realised it was forty years since I had seen them fresh and recently completed. The church still tells the story for those who can untangle the strands of imagination, fact, fantasy and legend - 'we see through a glass darkly' still.

We left Stiklestad in a sombre mood in the morning of that day at the end of July but petrol, coffee and sunshine soon restored us and it proved to be one of the most interesting days of my life.

I now quote directly from my personal diary written at the time –

> *"From Stiklestad Cultural Centre we took the main road and joined the E6 at Verdal, turned southwards and through industrial areas and over modern highways to turn left for Selbu and Røros. I did not recognise Selbu with its large lake until we reached the church as I am more used to the road from Trondheim a little further south. Selbu is renowned for its lovely flower-like knitting pattern which used to be included in all skiing gear and for the mill-stones they produced locally and exported to Trondheim and beyond in winter, down the frozen lake and river.*

> *We climbed up from Selbusjøen and it was coffee time. A little further up the road we pulled into the road side again. W O W !!!*

> *I was so over-awed that I could not take any photographs. My whole being was held enraptured by the panoramic view around me.*

> *'My God how wonderful Thou art, Thy majesty how bright, How beautiful Thy mercy's seat, In depths of burning light'* (Federick W. Faber 1814-63)

Selbu mittens.

We were on the lip of a circular plateau with a high rim of mountains completely encircling us in the far distance. It was all so bright and clear I imagined I could see the North Sea beyond the mountains to my left and the luscious valleys of Sweden over the rim to my right.

Our driver kindly phoned the Røros Tourist Board to enquire where we could find the elusive Aster Sibiricus so we were able to make a direct detour to grant my wish. We turned off the main Røros road to the right and drove along the north shore of the lake Aursunden passing several farms, south facing over the lake collecting sunshine when possible and a boat for local fishing. We found our goal.

Inspecting the four plants which had survived.

I was told of the rarity of this plant in winter 2002. I had mentioned it in 'A Vivid Shaft of Northern Light' connecting it then with Røros and wondering if Linnaeus or Gunnerus had heard of it through Jens Finne Borchegrevink, the parson/botanist born and brought up in Røros who had worked and studied with both of them. (Røros is one of the few places Linnaeus had visited in Norway)

Jorunn Sakrisvoll is a delightful middle-aged lady who was so grateful to have people genuinely interested in her plants. She is very concerned about the conservation of the aster. As we walked down the lane towards the lake she told us how she had voluntarily taken over the care of the plants from her father-in-law on the farm beside a ness on Lake Aursunden. She recalled how the family had made a stone path beside the beach on the spit of land where the children played and they were told not to go any further. They knew there were unusual plants there but they did not know what they were or how they came there and no where else.

The damming of the lake at the western outflow to the River Glåma for hydro electric power in 1922 caused a change in the water level and drifting ice. Consequently the aster population gradually decreased

The protected lake-side bed of Aster Siberica.

Siberian Aster

Cautiously and persistently the family have quietly worked to strengthen the banking, building a retaining wall to deal with the changing depth and flow of the lake. But why should this plant be found only here?'

(End of diary entry excerpt)

The plants were already known as *'asters'* in 1874 but they were not recognised as rarities until 1897 when Thekla H. Resvoll, according to Røros literature, identified the species as *Siberian aster*. It is known in Norway as *sibirstjerne*. I found on a polar expedition last year that the species is prevalent throughout the Arctic Circle in June and July (we were too late in Greenland and Iceland in September).

Curious to know more of the botanist who had recognised the specimen in Norway I found the intriguing biographies of two remarkable women, sisters born in Vågå, near Lom, on the edge of the Jotunheimen Mountains. Thekla Resvoll (1871-1948) was a pioneer of Norwegian botany with a particular interest in mountain plants in the Swiss Alps and Germany and around her home. She was one of the first women members of the academic staff of the Royal Frederik's University (now University of Oslo) 1902 – 1936. The Alpine Garden at Kongsvoll was commenced by Hannah in 1924 and a Vågå type soap-stone memorial to her stands in the garden now cared for by the NTNU Natural History Department.

Hanna Resvoll-Holmsen (1873-1943) was Thekla Resvoll's younger sister and also a botanist. To complicate nomenclature matters they were married to two brothers, the younger sister to the elder brother, Holmsen. Hanna was an academic late-developer, due to illness in her teens, and entered the Royal Frederik's University in 1900. She was a member of the expedition, led by Prince Albert of Monaco, the oceanographer, to Svalbard in 1907. In 1908 Hanna returned to Svalbard alone, taking only a tent, provisions, colour photographing equipment, a vasculum (*botaniserkasse*) and a gun. She produced the first illustrated flora of Svalbard in 1927 and by that time she was an assistant in the university botanical geography department.

It was like solving a mathematical theorem in my youth, determining who first identified the *Aster siberica*, but considering (our maths master always began by saying, 'Now let us consider …') her knowledge and experience of Svalbard there is no doubt it was Hanna M. Resvoll-Holmsen. This was later proved in contemporary, learned writings. Hannah did research in the forestry areas of the Norwegian mountains and became unpopular amongst the foresters because she advocated the replanting of birch trees and not spruce. Time has proved her correct and she is hailed as 'the first green stocking' long before the modern ecological ideas were predominant.

The geologist Adolf Hoel and botanist Hanna Resvoll-Holmsen were the driving forces behind the designation of the first conservation area in Svalbard. In the last few years the Svalbard Global Seed Vault has been established in the permafrost mountains near Longyearbyen. Duplicate seeds are stored from collections round the globe in a vaulted underground cavern, an 'insurance' against large scale regional or global crises.

The reference to Adolf Hoel reminds my dear amanuensis of a personal meeting, a natural science event, in late autumn 1938. The sudden late autumn storm gush of waters from high snow clad Lesja hurrungane mountains, flushed down the embanked road and rail track, filling all hollows and forcefully washing away the road and

ASTER SIBIRICUS
N. Sibirstjerne

Kongsvoll

the rail ballast leaving the rails suspended, with sleepers attached. A deep impassable flood was caused in Lesja.

It happened that Adolf Hoel had arrived on the last summer trip from Svalbard on the coal-bearing NSB's only vessel. On this occasion Hoel was in charge of another cargo, which could not be left behind in Åndalsnes with the coal, a consignment of musk oxen for Dovrefjell. The crates of animals, loaded on a lorry, were conveyed safely to the edge of the deep flood near Lesja railway station but no further. The road was impassable.

The messenger boy, in his black waterproof cape, had to hastily use the lines man's *dressin* (three wheeled cycle used normally on the rails) to rush to and from the flood with telephone messages to stop trains from Oslo, Dombås, Åndalsnes, so the station master could arrange alternative transportation. Meanwhile the crates of musk ox were being manually carried through the deep, flowing flood waters which the lorry could not traverse, and loaded onto another lorry on dry land. With relief the animals were away to Dovre leaving an unforgotten chaos to be cleared by railway and transport workers through the night. Dr Hoel's anxiety about the welfare of the animals from ice-cold Svalbard, possibly over rough arctic waters and then up Romsdal to be faced by flood waters, was understandable. They must have survived for there are still musk ox round Kongsvoll, the pilgrims' shelter on Dovrefjell.

To return to the present day in Aursunden and its unique Norwegian botanical situation, is interesting from a historical point of view. *Aster sibiricus* was one of the first four plants in Norway to be protected by law in 1915. Many botanists from Europe were being particularly attracted to the Dovre area from 1905 and it was feared the rare flowers were gleaned detrimentally to the natural area. The protection was lifted in 1921 for the hydro-electric scheme to permit the movement of the plant and restored in 1922. A further decree of 1981 declared *Aster sibiricus* should be protected throughout Norway.

But are the flowers we see in July-August really *Aster sibiricus?* The flowers we now see have all developed from one 'mother plant' which survived and gave off four shoots, which did not flower because they were not pollinated. Jorunn, innocent and motherly, has pollinated them (artificial insemination?) by drying the complete complex flower heads and sowing the seeds in the spring. Plants have been tried in similar areas but have not thrived. Will they survive in Røros if nobody tends them? '*God moves in a mysterious way His wonders to perform ...*' (William Cowper, 1731-1800). The delightful and accurate painting of *Aster sibiricus* by Dagny Tande Lid was certainly painted on the spot we know near Glåmos.

Aster sibiricus, the Norwegian *sibirstjerne*, is now named *Eurybia sibirica*. I should like to know the recognised botanical initials of the botanist who first described *Eurybia sibirica* as we have L. for Linnaeus.

We continued our pilgrimage that July day from Stiklestad to Røros and over lunch had the excitement of discovering one special member of our party was a descendant of Jens Finne Borschgrevink (1737-1819), the colleague of Gunnerus. I was able to point out the charity school, across the road from the Vardshus, which had been erected in 1799 by Jens Finne's aunt, Catherine Borchgrevink.

A present day descendant at the entrance to Catherine Borchgrevink's Charity School now the church office. 2009

Røros 'new' church (1784). March 2002

Upper portion of scree.

South-facing scree of the canyon Jutulhøgget.

My diary continues:

'We were not sure where we were going or why! We turned left up a non-descript road from the main Glåmå valley and climbed hairpin bends through wooded mountain terrain and over a brow to a car park. There had not been any spectacular scene on the way. Then we spotted a signpost pointing out the way to Information. It was a very difficult step-like path, over rocks and ancient tree roots. It was an awful (awe full, as well) sight that met our gaze — an extensive stone quarry, high and deep, fearful and tremendous, gaping at our feet. An ideal setting for vicious troll stories! The gigantic blocks of stone on the sides, with a few cave-like gaps and a dry massive stoned bottom, were so reminiscent of natural and terrorist disasters but on a larger scale. JUTULHOGGET is one of the longest canyons in Europe, a wild cleft 2.5km long and 200m deep. The deepest part of the canyon is 48m lower than the almost parallel River Glåmå.

Wonderful sunsets over quiet mountain roads – Friisveien, Vinge way to Ringebu and so home to Lillehammer.'

(End of diary extract for 25th July 2008)

There was so much to ponder over on the day's scene that a further visit, ten days later, was necessitated. It was not so fearful for I had gleaned a little more knowledge of the situation. There were some elm trees on a south facing slope I should like to have found but the way was too difficult for an ancient Briton. I wonder if there is some time relationship between *Aster sibiricus* and Jutulhogget? I am told that the canyon was created by the rupture of the dam of a proglacial lake. There had obviously been a powerful, earth shattering time for the great blocks of stone did not appear

Even the harsh rock provides "home" for "stone-crop".

weathered. As the 3-4km thick ice sheet melted and moved could a rock basined lake have been left behind after thousands of years? Was this Lake Aursunden whose only outflow is on the west, the Glåmå River with a bed 48m higher than the bottom of Jutulhogget? Could our flower have been dormant for thousands of years in the silt from a glacier of the north? Perhaps it was dispersed by a bird after all.

South facing scree seen through gap in massive ice-cut stone. 2009

Gudbrandsdalen - Lovers Lane

Over the mountains from the Eastern Valleys we come to the historic valley of Gudbrandsdalen. It was down this valley that Bishop Gunnerus hurriedly travelled by horse-drawn coach in 1771 when summoned to Copenhagen by the Chief Minister of Denmark to advise on the restructuring of Copenhagen University. Gunnerus' enthusiasm was renewed, hoping here at last was the opportunity for a university to be established in Norway.

It would be a pleasant drive, mid-July, down this great valley and there would be time for some botanising as the bishop stopped overnight at some parsonage or pilgrims' inn. There are still remarkable guest houses, established more than four hundred years ago, some pre-Reformation, for this had been a pilgrim route from the 11th century martyrdom of King Olav II, and still is. It is cosy to stay at Kongsvoll, it has been discreetly modernised and foot and vehicular pilgrims enjoy the pleasant, old fashioned hospitality (at modern prices). Adjacent, beside the old worn footpath, one of the University of Trondheim's Botanical Gardens can be enjoyed on the hillside.

Toftgård

Gudbrandsdalen and river Lågen from south, near Lillehammer to Dovrefjell.

The source of the river Lågen flows south-east from Lesjaskogsvatnet.

Tofte is an outstanding old family farm set on the hillside well above the river and kept in remarkable condition. Between such farms were rough shelters of stones and trees where travellers could collect and spend a night.

The River Lågen has a most interesting, possibly unique, beginning. It flows from the southern end of a man constructed lake, Lesjaskogvatnet, and eventually reaches the Skagerrak, the sea between Norway and Denmark. The River Rauma flows from the northern end of Lesjaskogvatnet and down Romsdal through the high ski resort of Bjorli to Åndalsnes and Romsdalfjord to the North Sea. The dams had been built some four centuries ago to provide water power for the then important iron works.

So the Lågen flows south-east to Otta where it is joined by the River Otta from the Grotli watershed and the bicolour river continues for some distance before mingling into the icy-green waters of the Lågan to occupy Gudbrandsdalen.

At Ringebu the large wooden stave church stands distinctly. Built in the 13th century and extended in 1630-31 it is still in use. Søren Christian Sommerfelt lived in the parsonage here from 1827 to 1838 after being *sogneprest* (dean) in Saltdalen from 1818 to 1824.

It was in 1999 that I first 'met' Søren Christian Sommerfelt (1794 - 1838) at the entrance to the Junkerdalen National Park. A carved wooden figure of this botanist/priest looks over the main path and along the River Junker. As priest in Saltdalen he could indulge his childhood interest in botany and in 1826 he wrote a supplemental

The river Rauma begins it race down Romsdal from west of Lesjaskogsvatnet.

Lesja with the constant water spray protected by trees.

The rows of planted trees provide a natural barrier to the snow carrying winds and collect snow, a source of water to an area that would otherwise have been a windswept desert.

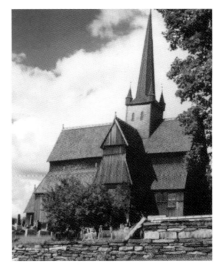

Ringbu stave church

131

Søren Christian Sommerfeldt (1794–1838).

Gudbrandsdalen towards Lake Mjøsa.

"Skiblander" the white swan of Mjøsa.

Flora lapponica which opened up interest in the protection of Junkerdalen. His personal herbarium is included in the University of Oslo Museum of Botany. I was disappointed there is no mention of him in Ringebu Church. I asked about his grave and was told. He was buried 'somewhere under the church floor'.

River, road and railway are again side by side down the fertile valley and still the route is E6 as we followed from Kirkenes. There are many small townships along the route and several small churches with large graveyards, for the narrow area has seen skirmishes for centuries. Holiday areas for playgrounds, caravans and *hytte* (cabins) abound especially where the valley broadens into lakes, first Losna, which narrows into the great Lake Mjøsa, the largest and longest lake in Norway. It still carries upon its waters the 150 year old paddle steamer, Skibladner, the world's oldest steamship still in operation. The treat is to go by rail from Lillehammer to Hamar and return by lake steamer, taking a traditional meal of steamed, fresh salmon and strawberries and cream. When I did the trip the best part was the local strawberries, early July Norwegian strawberries are superb, sweet, large and juicy, the best I have found in the world.

Lillehammer, now the largest town in Gudbrandsdal, clings to the eastern hillside before the Lake Mjøsa broadens to its widest stretch. The town was granted its charter in 1827, when its population numbered 55 - but its coat of arms tells of ancient history. It shows a skier (the only coat of arms in the world to show a skier) protecting the infant king with his shield as he hastily sped to safety over the snow covered mountains to the eastern valley from Gudbrandsdal. It was a time of civil strife and the precious burden was the child with royal blood. The skier was on his way to Trondheim and knew of the dangerous conditions ahead if he had proceeded up the valley and faced the Dovrefjell. The Birkebeiner (for his legs were covered with birch-bark, too poor for leather boots) was the fore-runner of the many thousands of people who now annually take part in the most famous Norwegian ski race from Rena to Lillehammer, each carrying the weight of a two and a half year old child in their rucksack.

In 1994 Lillehammer and the surrounding area was host to the Winter Olympic Games, a natural, most picturesque winter area. My friends, attending from Singapore said it was very, very cold and dark (they were sailors not skiers) but Norwegian friends said it was wonderful, most successful, in spite of years of arranging, planning and hard labour. It certainly changed Lillehammer. The establishment of many tracks and roadways, new bridges and special buildings for social activities, hospitality, filming and broadcasting, disrupted the pleasant country town dominated by *Maihaugen* (May Hill and the not to be missed Sandvig historic collection), for several years.

The aftermath has left a large vibrant town all the year round, the residents benefitting from the improved roads and housing, educationally renowned facilities and suppliers and shops. I still miss the old Storgata but the modern pedestrian way is an asset, cyclists the only danger. My favourite building 'left-over' and adapted from the Olympics is Nordre Ål Church. I understand it was a recreational centre for foreign participants in the games but now I find it a source of spiritual re-creation with its unusual 'lantern tower' of natural light incorporated above the almost circular nave. The beautiful 'Stations of the Cross' depicted on the north wall are astonishing, each one is an art gallery in itself, showing in details little associated

Lake Mjøsa can be seen (winter only) a grey blue line in the distance. Every true Lillehammer inhabitant insists his home must be within the sight of Mjøsa.

The Birkebeiner on the bridge over the Mesna river at Lilletorget.

Maihaugen

133

One of the fourteen stations of the Cross by Anne Lise Knoff in N. Ål Church. Every stroke of the brush has meaning. Each picture has a wild flower somewhere this delicate Harebell, Campanula rotundifolia, particularly delights me.

signs and objects we so easily forget. For me, the highlight is the inclusion of a different wild flower in each one.

I was captured by Gudbrandsdalen fifty years ago not only by the persuasive Norwegian travel agent in London but by Sigrid Undset's trilogy, 'Kristin Lavransdatter' set in this great valley. Sigrid Undset (1882-1949) was born in Kalunberg, Denmark, in the lovely red corner house in the little market place that was her mother's childhood home. I found it at the end of the street with the distinctive red brick cathedral at the other. I was looking for the five towers of the cathedral - each named after a female saint, one being St Gertrude.

Professor Undset (a renowned archaeologist) and family moved back to Norway when Sigrid was two years old. Her childhood was spent in Christiania (now Oslo) much attached to her ailing father. She moved to Lillehammer in 1919 ... her life and work are much too interesting to retell briefly and her influence too personally deeply felt to put into words. Sigrid Undset was awarded the Nobel Prize for Literature in 1928 ('Kristin Lavransdatter' published 1920-22). Details of the meticulous scientific and historical research she did and her personal books and papers were left to the Royal Norwegian Society of Science and Letters and are housed in Trondheim beside the Gunnerus Library. Bjerkebæk, her Lillehammer home and garden is newly restored and tells all.

One cross section of Lillehammer changes only with the seasons. It is the gash hacked deep in the hillside from the Nevrefjell area down to the joining of the River Lågen and Lake Mjøsa, ice-ages ago and worn and artistically crafted by water-powered time over millennia. Silt and glacial debris has somewhat levelled the upper area so there are numerous lakes, meandering streams and wet, boggy land eventually draining into the Mesna Lakes and dashing into the old cleft. But, like us, the waters pause for man has also been at work in recent centuries. The lakes have been dammed, channels cleared and installations control the flow of water over the Mesna Waterfalls and down the steep, stony cliffs and valley 510 metres to Lake Mjøsa and eventually the sea.

The cascading water is accompanied by a footpath through the trees and bushes along its banks. The path is often steep and uneven over tree roots and protruding rocks, there are some natural steps in places

Mesna Falls

Rainbow spray Mesna Falls.

Collett's Bridge over Mesna Falls.

The "dipper".

A waterfall, placid autumn strean of Mesna.

The same stream in winter when it is easily possible to cross the frozen river on foot.

and even an occasional, helpful hand-rail or barrier. The narrow way is well worn and usually accompanied by the flushing music of the gushing water. At every turn nature provides some pleasing scene of liquid silver water, fantastic rock slabs, smoothed grey stones and gnarled trees struggling for a foothold in the almost bare rock terrain, even tiny bushes attempting to cling to stones in a shallow, stagnant bend. You may even catch a glimpse of a diamond splattered rainbow especially after the biennial 'rinsing' of the river, an exciting sight we love to see. It takes place in spring and autumn when the dams are full. The flood gates are opened at a certain time and what may have been a mere trickle suddenly becomes a torrent of water sweeping dead and rootless vegetation away for other natural use.

Near the top of the waterfalls faithfully stands the elegant Collett's Bro (Bridge) the favourite subject of many artists. Frederik Jonas Lucian Bothfield Collett (1839 - 1914) himself was a well known artistic visitor to Lillehammer who frequently painted the Mesnali Falls. He persuaded local like-minded people that a bridge was needed at this point and the money was raised by small donations, 'kronerulling'. It is not surprising to be told that Collett was so keen to paint this beautiful scene in winter, when it was far too cold to sit outside with his easel, that he transported a small heated studio on a sledge to a convenient site. He frequently hid 'a dipper', a small bird to be found dipping in and out at the water's edge, in his paintings and this became his sign. Please notice the gold dippers on the bridges in Lilletorget, beside the town's coat of arms and give a thought to the artist who preserved natural beauty for later generations in his work. We return to the footpath from Collett's Bridge and continue down some fifty metres and turn round to obtain the best view of the bridge. The rough steep footpath leads eventually to a more level part and the stream slows and broadens into a bathing place. How my party of teenagers from Elland loved it forty years ago when staying at the Birkebeiner Youth Hostel. It is still popular. Here you can join the wider pathway, Fossveien, and continue the descent.

There is a wealth of wild flowers and grasses in the hedgerow beside the path and it is here, in due season, that you, if you look carefully, will find masses of one of my favourite flowers, *Linnea borealis*. It was from this spot I collected two specimens, to be pressed and mounted by my dear companion, to present to the Singapore Botanic Gardens on the occasion of the opening of the exhibition commemorating the tercentenary of the birth of Linnaeus. The fragile stem rises 3 to 4 cm above a net mat of tiny three lobed leaves and fine surface root system. Each stem gracefully bears two small bell-shaped pink/white twin flowers - its English common name Twin-flower. This is the flower the great botanist named after himself in 1732 - I like his sense of humour.

Linnea borealis, Fossveien, Lillehammer.

The path continues past a fairly modern hydroelectric power station, no longer in use. All modern workings are disguised by beautiful trees. The forceful water in the falls had been reused three times in the early part of the twentieth century but later developments created a more efficient means. The water is funnelled from the upper dams into deep underground tunnels beneath the waterfalls from Kanten, the edge of the plateau, to one powerful station at the bottom, beside the lake. All modern workings are concealed within the mountain.

Now permanently surfaced, the path passes beside ultra modern apartments occupying the land that was once a brewery, using the water and its own little power station. There are some lovely old birch trees clinging to the river bank here - a delight in every season and a foot bridge and some stepping stones at this point or you may con-

Spring-cleaning the Lillehammer streets.

Ulvarer

tinue down to Lilletorget and cross the road bridge. At the other side of the river steep steps lead down the bank side and the path continues.

Here we enter a scene of tranquility. The trees are dense, only leaves dapple the light above the again narrow path. Although we pass below three bridges, carrying roads and the railway, the sounds of a busy town are silenced by the constant, torrential, rushing waters. We can use two footbridges to recross and from the buildings concealed amongst the woods we realise this has been a woollen mill and imagine workers pattering across the bridges to bring their baskets of raw wool to be processed. It is peaceful, cool and so pleasant here these days, unbelieveable there are thousands of people nearby for we hardly ever meet any one.

I love this old path, 3.5 km long, from Kanten to my favourite shopping centre at Strandtorget beside Mjøsa, for it takes one through the ancient history of the area almost as clearly as Maihaugen shows it. Lovers' lane...?

Lake Mjøsa and Lillehammer in the background. (Photo Hoff)

Along the South Coast to Rjukan and on to Hardangervidda

W e fly with time (actually Tor's car) from Mjøsa through Eidsvoll (of historical significance in 1814) and Oslo, the capital city of the Kingdom of Norway, the seat of Government and Parliament (*Stortinget*) and the King, to take a peep at Southern Norway.

The small town of Oslo had gradually developed into a market place where valleys and sea met, still protected from the ferocious Skagerrak which separated Denmark, the ruling kingdom, from Norway. Its wooden buildings had been completely destroyed by fire and rebuilt fourteen times between 1,000 AD and 1624 when King Christian IV, king of Denmark and Norway is reputed to have said, *'Enough is enough!'* He pointed his gloved forefinger at a spot near the Akershus fortress and declared it should be the centre of a brick and stone built town to be known as Christiania in his honour.

Three hundred years later and no longer under Danish sovereignty, the name reverted to Oslo as we know it today. The impressive bronze statue of the gloved hand of King Christian IV, complete with lace trimmed gauntlet, marks the decisive spot in the old market place surrounded by a few buildings remaining from the seventeenth century.

Although the birthplace of Johan Ernst Gunnerus on 26th February 1718, we will not linger in the modern capital city dominated by its red-brick City Hall on the quayside head of the busy Oslofjord. The Royal Palace keeps its eyes on the still eloquent Karl Johan's Gate and the aging golden yellow building of the Storting. We will move into Sørlandet, the area of Southern Norway, towards Kristiansand, a later town planned by King Christian IV - king of Denmark and Norway.

Oslo City Hall and Pipervika from A/S Midnatsol January 2005.

Many times I have visited the South Coast of Norway with its protecting chain of rocks and islands bordering the northern coast of the Skagerrak. All the Bergen Line Steamers (BDS) from Newcastle to Bergen called in at Stavanger in the nineteen fifties and sixties. From my first visit in 1952 I remember only my thankfulness in reaching *terra firma* after the North Sea crossing on M/S Venus. The Fred Olsen ships called in at Kristiansand on the way to their home port of Oslo from Newcastle. Passengers could go ashore a short while and it was possible to admire the clear cut lines and crossings of the design of the city within its square boundary. On two occasions we have had the privilege of sailing from Bergen to Oslo on M/V Midnatsol and anchoring beside Akersus Castle facing the City Hall clock.

Stavanger has become a world famous oil depot in the last three decades . Kristiansand is a very busy transportation ferry link with Europe through Denmark, a level country with uninterrupted kilometres of motor ways.

Akershus Castle Oslo 2005.

The hinterland of the twin counties of Aust (East) and Vest (West) Agder, whose southern coast I had frequently seen from sea and air, was a complete surprise. My first real visit was in August 2008. We speeded down Gudbrandsdal and by evening we reached Drammen leaving dull, grey, damp weather behind. Drammen will always be an important paper producing town in my mind. Here I had been taken round a paper mill some thirty years ago. I was intrigued by the similarity in manufacture between paper and the woollen cloth industry in my native West Riding of Yorkshire, England. Very similar machinery was used in both instances. Now wool has almost been replaced by synthetic man-made fibres and I presume there have been changes in the paper making process. Has timber been preserved?

Christen Smith (1785-1816)

I had passed through Drammen by train several times and was aware of the vast timbering industry in the region. Christen Smith (1785-1816) was the son of a wealthy Drammen merchant and even as a child a keen amateur botanist. He studied medicine in Copenhagen and practised there for a time. In 1814 came the opportunity he longed for - he was appointed the first professor of Botany at Christiania (now Oslo) University with the responsibility for the organisation of the Botanic Garden there. In preparation for the new position he spent some pioneering months in the Canary Islands with a German botanist, Leopold von Buch, and made detailed studies of many aspects of natural science, intending to write these up in England before returning to Norway. However Sir Joseph Banks persuaded him to go as botanist and geologist on his expedition sent to the Congo and there he died in 1816 without transcribing his earlier notes or actually taking up his professorship.

"Smith belonged to a group of distinguished men where one could feel the influence of the spirit of Linné. Among those men should Smith forever be mentioned with honour and glory as a martyr of the science".

Arendal

So wrote his friend and field companion, Leopold von Buch. Several plants, mainly from the Canary Islands, have the epithet, 'smithii,' commemorating the discoveries and recordings of this young scientist.

Clear of the city and the once very busy ports and homes of affluent traders and builders, the countryside opened out. There were no steep valley sides and the rolling pasture lands supported a dairying industry. The forests were not dense and dark but the bands of woodland revealed a myriad shades of pleasant green. At one moment we had a vivid, glowing sunset gradually declining into soft grey/mauve on our right hand side whilst on the left, a peep of moonlight, like a watchful eye awaiting the opportunity to rise from the sea, low on the horizon.

The evening of the next day (16.08.2008), was even more exquisite in a different way. Our delicious evening meal of handcaught local mackerell in home-made fish cakes was longer than it might have been for we kept leaving the table to see the position of the shadow of the earth almost completely covering the moon at 11.08pm exactly. The lunar eclipse was very beautiful from the flagged terrace, hillside platform with a foreground of sparse pines silhouetted against a cloudless, black sky.

We entered the coastal town of Arendal by ferry from the island of Tromøy, a most picturesque approach on a bright sunny day. The brilliance of the bright colours against the white buildings dazzled us as we walked along the sea front to the mouth of the River Nid and the bustling fish market. The inner harbour is Pollen, once a major shipping centre, now a jolly meeting place to suit all tastes and many holiday craft; an up-to-date rival for Venice, I thought, as I looked for a gondolier!

There had been a market in Arendal from 1723 and an important, wealthy south coast port for shipbuilding, and the export of timber, ironwork and mineral ores. The larger islands fringing the coast made ideal winter harbours when ships were stranded sailing from the Kattegat through Skagerrak to the North Sea and the outer world. Fortunes fluctuated but by 1939 the fourth largest Nowegian tanker fleet was based at Arendal. The sailors' island havens have become summer residences for the thousands of Norwegians who have kept the sunny, sandy beaches and rocky coves secret.

Leaving the sand-dune hidden coast behind, we were soon into the far stretching, rollling farming country again. This was not Norway! It was Denmark. I realised Copenhagen was much closer to Sørlandet than to Trondheim, Denmark even easier to reach than Bergen. Similarly 'the Four hundred years' night', (*Firehundreårsnatten*, Henrik Ibsen in 'Peer Gynt') domination of Danish sovereignty did not take into account the country and people north of a southern belt from Oslo/Christiania to Stavanger.

Bishop Gunnerus forcibly realised the existence of this barrier when he reached Copenhagen early October 1771 at the request of the Chief Minister, to advise on the reorganisation of Copenhagen University. Excitedly Gunnerus had sent a short letter to his friend Linnaeus in Uppsala on 3rd October informing him of his arrival in Copenhagen. He had already visited the young king, Christian VII (1749-1808) and Queen Caroline Mathilde (1751-1779) and glimpsed some copperplates being prepared for the second part of '*Flora Norvegica*'. Linnaeus replied on 26th October that he was disappointed Gunnerus could not visit him on his journey to Copenhagen, the friends had never actually met, but he insisted he must see **gunnera** in the botanical nursery in Copenhagen.

Fjære kirke

Rjukan

Details of roof and sidedoor of Heddal Church.

By mid-December Gunnerus had submitted his suggestions for the reorganisation of Copenhagen University to include a Norwegian University, as quietly envisaged by the learned society in Trondheim for a decade. Some interest was shown but the new university could not possibly be in Trondheim for that was too far away for the still Germanic dominated Danish Court. Gunnerus realized that a possible Norwegian establishment would only be considered no further north than Kristiansand, easily accessible to Danes.

December-January 1772 saw political turmoil in Copenhagen. The reforms of the Chief Minister, Johnann Friedrich Stuensee (1731 -1772) being carried out without time for opposition, alienating many officials, resulted in a conspiracy during a court ball in January 1772. Struensee was arrested and later publically, brutally executed, the accusation being his liaison with Queen Caroline Mathilde.

Gunnerus was terribly disappointed about the turn of events and the failure of his plans. He longed to return to Trondheim and leave the political turmoil behind. He wrote to Linnaeus on 29 February 1772 of his desire to be away from the capital but he hoped there were still some in authority who might help but they proved afraid of the diminution of Danish power by extending academic knowledge to Norway. He reached Norway on 1st July and wrote to Suhm in Copenhagen, '*I am heartily glad to be home and never wish to see Copenhagen again.*' His nephew who had been part of the Trondheim family for ten years said his uncle was no longer amusing and cheerful but quiet and morose. Was this the beginning of the end?

From Kristiansand and Sørlandet we make our way northwards up interesting, gradually deepening valleys. Setesdal with its unique black felt bunad trimmed with bright red and green, divides the counties of Agder into East and West from the edge of the Hardanger mountain plateau to the Skagerrak. Nidelva, the river with its mouth at Arendal, twists its way through lakes, canals, farmlands and deciduous forest areas, revealing some old ironworks and pottery, to its sources in Telemark.

At Rjukan, on the edge of the Hardangervidda National Park, is the great hydro-electric power station and electrochemical processing plant almost entirely concealed by nature. The town was founded by the industrialist Sam Eyde, (1866-1940), who was born near Arendal. The one main street in Rjukan is named Sam Eydes gate. The sabotage of the heavy water during WWII survives in the accounts and film of 'The Heroes of Telemark'. Now a winter sports centre the distinctive mountain Gaustatoppen (1,883m) provides a splendid background.

Packed nitrogen fertilizer ready for distribution and use by landowners. This special product of Rjukan is extracted from the air by the readily available hydro-electric power.

Gaustatoppen (1,883 m)

The restored Heddal Church.
The largest stave church in Norway.

In the neighbourhood is the magnificently, recently renovated, Heddal Stave Church. Towards Oslo is the silver city of Kongsberg. Silver mining was carried out in this area from 1623 when the mineral was reputedly accidentally found by two children and their ox. King Christian IV of Denmark and Norway visited the following year and named the mines, Kongsberg. The area is well worth going over carefully but we must not tarry further here but press onwards over the mountains in search of the answer to my riddle. Where did Johan Ernst Gunnerus die?

The Heart of the Matter -
A Matter of the Heart

My pilgrimage now takes me back to the beginning. I take flight over the Hardangervidda, Northern Europe's most extensive mountain plateau. Amongst the impressive mountain tarns and lakes, around dramatic grey landscapes, a small footpath worn by centuries of travellers, can be seen with patches of moss and sturdy mountain bushes in the crevices. The plateau falls steeply to the west, the rivers are short with powerful waterfalls en route for the fjords of western Norway, especially the Hardangerfjord.

The monks from Lyse Abbey, near Bergen, had a grange in Ullensvang on Sørfjord which could be reached easily by boat on the Hardangerfjord. Here they kept sheep, the shorn wool being taken back to the abbey or sold and the meat being preserved in ice. I suspect the name Ullensvang may have come from this ness by the church when the sheep had been shorn and fleece been packed into boats or sold. (Translated it could be 'the wool field').

There were also apple orchards - the beginning of the fruit growing industry in Hardanger which survives today.

Flying over Hardangervidda in June.

Mountain path over Hardangervidda and shelter.

Narrow road with steep drop on fjord side.

The monks had built steep steps into the mountain side to aid their ascent of the mountain block - still there today.

The sea and fjord waterways remained open for centuries, footpaths and animal tracks wellworn, until the turn of the twentieth century and the development of motorised vehicles. Paths were often little more than cliff shelves above the fjord. I love to hear Magnhild tell of the English lady driving to Odda shortly after WWII. She was terrified of driving on the righthand side so near the cliff/fjord edge that she drove down the centre of the narrow road. This stopped traffic in both directions until a friendly policeman sorted the congestion and personally guided her safely into Odda.

Later decades in the twentieth century have seen many advantageous civil engineering projects instigated and completed. Tunnels have been constructed in places often closed by snow in winter or to make a shorter route through the mountains than round a narrow fjord edge. Road bridges have been built providing permanent highways often replacing ferries.

A driving force, in the provision of safe and binding conditions on highways, byways and islands, has been a member of the Storting, Kjell Olav Opseth, Minister of Transport and Communicatons 1990 - 1996 and Minister of Local Government Affairs 1996-7. Opseth (1936-) represented his home area of Førde for two decades. He was a practical politician who knew from experience the need for tunnels and bridges to bond the country together all the year round. The operation includes the Lærdal Tunnel, 24,500m, the longest road tunnel in the world and unusual in the provision of a well-lit stopping area partway through.

Neat fruit orchards of Lofthus.

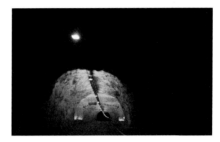

Lærdal Tunnel aproaching rest-area.

Wild roses beside Sørfjord, Ullensvang Church on ness in background.

The monks' steps helping the climb over to Hamar and Hovedøy.

Lyse Abbey Cloisters

Kværnes old stave church.

The Monks' steps on to the vidda.

Our flight continues north-west to Stad, the most westerly point of Norway where I started this musing. This time we will continue north east along the coast line passing the delightful old fishing village of Bud, above the rough patch of sea, Hustadvika, which we know made Gunnerus very sick, and turn into Kvernesfjorden to rest at Kvernes on the southern tip of the island of Averøy. Today we can go all the way by road - modern engineering has joined several island to the main-land and each other. The long bridge, parallel to Hustavika, is fantas-tic, 'the Atlantic Highway' - I consider it one of the wonders of modern Norway.

Eighteenth century shipping maps of this area show Kvernes as the most important town in the area, certainly the old stave church there was the dominant meeting place. It remains apparently propped up, as it has for several centuries, beside the 'modern' nineteenth century white painted larger church. There are traces of pre-Christian burials on the site.

Gunnerus rested at Kvernes some days, either on his ship or at the par-sonage. I have surveyed the site several times hoping for inspiration but I have been met by 'fire' at every turn - the parsonage had been burnt down in the early nineteenth century including all the church records, archives had been lost during war-time bombing ... The bishop's party moved towards Trondheim, in the Kristiansund area. We can deduce with some certainty that he was on his ship but what was the name of the ship? To whom did it belong? No vessel was mentioned amongst his goods and he died in debt. The illness must have been far more seri-ous than seasickness. There are suggestions in his nephew's letter (Nils Dorph Gunnerus) to Carl von Linné that he had been suffering some time from piles but few illnesses were diagnosed in the eighteenth cen-tury. His earthly journey must have been completed. "Thy will be done".

At last, after all the fiery denials the church book of Kristiansund 1773 was discovered. The Register of deaths included that of His Grace the Bishop Johannes Ernestus Gunnerus on a visitation journey. Set on a copy of two full pages of the register from January 1773 to March 1774 the actual entry for 25th September 1773 is marked in red and then enlarged above:

This still does not answer my question where? Kristiansund, Kvernes, scattered over several islands and what about the boat?

I returned to Trondheim from a joyfully uplifting time with friends in Romsdal early July 2008. We traversed again the coastal road from Molde (now a bishop's seat) over the Atlantic Highway to Kvernes, Kristiansund and Trondheim and there rested on the site of Gunnerus' home (Britannia Hotel).

The Atlantic Highway – it is a bridge not a precipice!

Excerpt from the church book in Kristiansund 1773 - Register of deaths. The text reads: "Den 25 September døede her Hans Højærværdighed Biscopen HE^r* Johannes Ernestus Gunnerus paa Visitations-Rejsen p. 55.. 7. " which translates into: On 25th September his Grace Bishop HE*^{r}* Johannes Ernestus Gunnerus died here on visitation journey, after 55 years 7 months.*

The Atlantic Highway joining islands and making a remarkable bridgeway avoid the rough sea parch of Hustadvik.

Kværnes 1826

On Thursday, 3 July 2008 I found J. E. Gunnerus, alive, well and active in Trondheim, of course!

Considering time and ages as I gazed on Romsdalshorn the previous days, its 'horn' ever pointing sharply upwards, I realised man's life span was infinitesimal in God's creation. It did not matter where Gunnerus died if his influence for good lives on.

I have found evidence in many places of associations with Johan Ernst Gunnerus, of his thoughts, involvements, development of knowledge and his application of experience in the revelation of God the Creator in the microscopic and mighty, the simple and significant, the beautiful and beneficial. In the world wide web of modern technology we have the spiritual contact without visible connections.

I stood on the quayside in Trondheim that July day and gazed at the name plate, 'R/V GUNNERUS' (R/V: Research/Vessel). How wonderful to find the naturalist/bishop still in evidence on the fjord, doing the work which fascinated him, although difficult 250 years ago. There in the city which has now the university of which he dreamed - though it must have been a somewhat different dream in his earthly days.

Quotation from my diary, Thursday, July 3rd 2008:

We went down to the quayside to meet the NTNU vessel coming in to dock. There was some problem about making the gangway safe for me to climb on board. I was so determined to stand on R/V Gunnerus that I think I could have flown! The problem was safely and comfortably resolved by the use of a metal door or plate from ground level to boat and solid steps on board.

We were given a hearty welcome. There were no students on board but the captain and the 'master' made up for a crowd. Captain Arve Knutsen officially welcomed the small party on board, arranged by the Gunnerus Librarian, and introduced the marine biologist in charge, Jon Arne Sneli. They were most enthusiastic about their work.

It was a pleasure to be with 'Gunnerus'. The NTNU based vessel operates mainly in the Trondheimsfjord, frequently around Hitra (Agdenes). They spend 220 days a year at sea, a maximum of 25 students with them at work from 8am to 8pm. Regular measurements are taken and detailed record kept of salinity, temperature and conditions. The ship contained the most up to date electronic equipment. We saw the long, snake-like metres of wire and tubing and the circular chamber with dynamic monitoring equipment to stay still when it was lowered beneath the boat. The underwater camera was controlled by a 750m cable data line.

I was most interested to learn that much of the equipment had been designed and produced by present day technicians with the Kongsberg Electronics Companies who had been ex-students. This ship was their beloved 'alma mater' and their interest remained, developed in fostering present day students, unconsciously passing on Gunnerus' silver spirit.

The original research vessel was commissioned in 1921 mainly to transport whole live fish for research. In 1940-45 it was taken over by the Germans and not restored until 1962. The present vessel 'Gunnerus' was taken into operation in March 2006. It is a fully equipped oceanological purpose built vessel with thirty square metres deck space and forty four metres long. After much discussion about the naming of the vessel, the enthusiastic, knowledgeable marine biologist

Gunnerus approached

Professor Sneli & Gunnerus Librarian.

Munkholmen from r/v Gunnerus.

committee member, J. Arne Sneli suggested 'Gunnerus' and it was accepted. I consider professor Sneli was divinely inspired to so spread and deepen the enthusiasm and knowledge Johan Ernst Gunnerus found in God's word written in Nature.

(End of diary extract for Thursday, July 3rd 2008)

But the pilgrimage does not end there. I remember my dear old aunt used to say, in her native Yorkshire dialect, and I guess that included many old viking words, '*Sammer 'em up and 'ugger 'em in*.' The translation I was given as a child was, '*Pick them up and carry them*'. In other words, get on with the task in hand! Let us collect the inspiration and knowledge for good of such forbears as Gunnerus, lift it to our day and generation and pass it on, as we have found it being done now on Trondheim's Fjord.

Fremad!
F R A M !

The Pilgrims Rest at Linton-in-Wharfedale, June 2009.　　(*Photo Nyhus*)

Let my vision, Lord, be keen and clear this day;
Clear the air is when mists have blown away;
Show my upward searching eyes
Sunlit peaks and cloudless skies,
To the summit turn my eyes this day.

Give me courage, Lord, to face the long ascent;
Sense to follow where others safely went;
Give me wisdom, Lord, to read
Map and compass in my need;
Give me comrades for the long ascent.

Free to falter, Lord, we meet the challenge still;
Not for us, Lord, the lounging laggard will;
Though the mountain hides in mist,
We shall stumble to its crest;
When we reach it, climb a higher still.

Some are starting now and some have gained the height;
All are comrades who keep the end in sight;
All who take Thee as their guide,
Turn not back nor turn aside;
They shall stand their on the sunlit height.

Frederick Pratt Green.

The author's hand-writing in 1952. This hymn of the Reverend Pratt Green (1903–2000) had just been published in the New Sunday School Hymn Book of the Methodist Church and I was just setting out for Norway with three cousins. Our minister suggested we should adopt this as our theme song. This piece of paper actually came on that journey and many more. In 1965 and 1967 I brougt large parties of teenage students to Norway and again we used it in our daily worship. By this time I had met Frederick Pratt Green at an annual Methodist Conference and he gave me per-mission to use it any time. He was especially delighted that it should be used in Norway and wished to come with us. His papers are collected in Durham University (my alma mater too).

Bibliography

Aase, M. 1998. Biskop i beste opplysningsånd. Forskningspolitikk 21, 12-13.

Aase, M. and M. Hård 1998. "Det norska Aten" Trondheim som lærdomsstad under 1700-tallets andra hälft. "Athens of the North" : Trondheim as an intellectual environment in the second half of the 18th century. Lychnos 1998, 37- 74.

Blunt, W. 1971. The compleat naturalist : a life of Linnaeus. London, Collins, 256 p.

Cooper, A. H. 1907. The Norwegian fjords. London, Adam and Charles Black, 178 p.

Dahl, O. 1892-1911. Biskop Gunnerus' virksomhed fornemmelig som botaniker: tilligemed en oversigt over botanikens tilstand i Danmark og Norge indtil hans død. Trondhjem, 5 vol.

A Dictionary of eighteenth-century history. 2001. Edited by J. Black and R. Porter. London, Penguin, 880 p.

Engegård, G. 1973. Biskop Gunnerus og "Flora Norvegica". Blyttia 31, 3- 15.

Gunnerus, J. E. 1758. Hans opvækkelige Hyrdebrev til det velærværdige, høj- og vellærde Præsteskab i Tronhjems Stift. Trondhjem, Jens Christensen Winding, 40 p.

Gunnerus, J. E. 1761-1772. Brevveksling 1761-1772. Johan Ernst Gunnerus og Carl von Linné; utgitt av Leiv Amundsen; med bistand av Rolf Nordhagen og Erling Sivertsen. Trondheim, Universitetsforlaget, 205 p.

Gunnerus, J. E. 1776-1772. Jo. Ern. Gunneri Flora Norvegica : observationibus praesertim oeconomicis, panosque norvegici locupletata. Nidrosiae, Typis Vindingianis, 2 vol.

Gunnerus, J. E. 1997. Hans opvækkelige Hyrde-brev. Trondheim, Universitets-biblioteket i Trondheim, 40 p. Facsimilia Bibliothecae Universitatis Nidrosiensis: 1.

Hansen, T. 1964. Arabia felix : the Danish expedition of 1761-1767. London, Collins, 381 p.

Haugen , Einar, *Norsk-Engelsk Ordbok*, Oslo: Universitetsforlaget 1965

Hohnen, D. 2000. Hamlet's castle and Shakespeare's Elsinore. Copenhagen, Christian Ejlers. 116 p.

Linné, C. von. 1732. Lappland resa år 1732. Edited by M. von Platen and C-O. von Sydow. Stockholm, 276 p.

De Maré, E. 1952. Scandinavia: Sweden, Denmark, and Norway. London, Batsford, 262 p.

Marsh, Gertrude M., *A Vivid Shaft of Northern Light*. Trondheim: Tapir 2002

Mee Arthur, *King's England* Derbyshire: Hodder & Stoughton 1936

Mossberg, B. 1995. Gyldendals store nordiske flora. Oslo, Gyldendal, 695 p.

Munck, T. 1990. Seventeenth century Europe : state, conflict and the social order in Europe, 1598-1700. Houndmills, Macmillan, 457 p.

Munthe, Preben, Christen Smith, *Biography of Christen Smith*, Norway 2004

Printz, H. 1918. Biskop J.E. Gunnerus som botaniker. Pp. 79-96 in: Johan Ernst Gunnerus 1718-26. Februar-1918. Mindeblade utgitt av det Kongelige Norske Videnskabers Selskab. Trondheim.

Rundo, Svein, *Geiranger Kyrke 150 År*, Geiranger 1985

Slingsby, Willam Cecil, *Norway, the Northern Playground*, Edinburgh: David Douglas 1904

Stagg, F. N. 1952. North Norway : a history. London, Allen & Unwin, 205 p.

Stagg, F. N. 1953. The heart of Norway : a history of the central provinces. London, Allen & Unwin, 194 p.

Stagg, F. N. 1954. West Norway and its fjords : a history of Bergen and its provinces. London, Allen & Unwin, 245 p.

Stagg, F. N. 1956. East Norway and its frontier : a history of Oslo and its uplands. London, Allen & Unwin, 285 p.

Stearn, W. T. 1992. Botanical Latin : history, grammar, syntax, terminology, and vocabulary. Devon, David & Charles, 546 p.

Stearn, W. T. 1994. Stearn's dictionary of plant names for gardeners : a handbook on the origin and meaning of the botanical names of some cultivated plants. London, Cassell, 363 p.

Sowerby, James, *English Botany*, London: Printed for the Author by J.Davies 1790

Til opplysning : Universitetsbiblioteket i Trondheim 1768-1993. University Library of Trondheim 1768-1993. 1993. Edited by H. Nissen and M. Aase. Trondheim, Tapir, 287 p. Det Kongelige norske videnskabers selskab. Skrifter. 1993: 1.

Trondheim : one thousand years in the city of St. Olav. 1992. Edited by J. Sandnes et al. Trondheim, Strindheim trykkeris forlag, 70 p.

Trondheims historie : 997-1997. 1996-1997. Edited by J. Sandnes et al. Oslo, Universitetsforlaget, 6 vol.

Wagner, P. 1990. Icones Florae Danicae. Flora Danicas "Urteteignere" og Illumniationsskolen for Quindekiønnct". Pp. 93- 100 in: Blomster fra sans og samling. København, Rhodos, 221 p.

Acknowledgements

The author wishes to express her deep gratitude to all who have 'helped her on her pilgrim way' from Yorkshire, Norway, Singapore, Warwickshire, Western Australia, Pole to Pole and intermediate stations and to those friends who have passed this way before, gone but not forgotten.

I am deeply indebted to Tor Arnesen and Ørnulf Norgård without whose advice, knowledge and persistent encouragement this work would never have been completed.

To Anthony Sofroniou, Clare and John Wright, Stein Johansen, Per Halstein Nielsen, Anna Sylvia Kielsen Nielsen, Reidar and Hanna Berit Hoff, Tulla Maelhum, Thor Olsen, Hanne Mari Nyhus, Finn Helge Nustad, Geir Midtun, David C. Bridgwater, Sir Peter Rigby and his Mallory Courtiers (on wheels), Hege Kolberg (and GAs), Else Kristine and Inger Johanne - the Mermaids and their related staff on MS Midnatsol and MV Fram, Nils Einar Stenstø, Jon-Arve Sneli, Ioan and Sandra Morgan, Alan Parton, Svein Runde, Karl Mjelva, Edmund H. Utne, Bjørn Langlien, Francis Thyer, Christopher Power, Torbjørn Lefstad, Mari Røstvold, Anntin and Rasmus Sunde, Helen and Erling Finne, Jorunn Sakrisvoll and you - the reader.

For help you have given me in unrecognised ways, broad and narrow, sometimes in the ditch as well as the mountain top, for patience and practical help, I would present my sincere thanks and hope you will enjoy the result with a smile, a tear and much happiness.

Illustrations

All illustrations, maps and pictures throughout the book are by the author except where otherwise stated.

Special thanks are given to John, Rebecca, David and staff of the Heaton-Cooper Studio Grasmere as indicated.

The author gives very special thanks to Mari Røstvold for discovering, recovering and working so wonderfully ' St Gertrude's pilgrim'.